# The Car Design Yearbook **2**

Stephen Newbury

# The Car Design Yearbook 2

the definitive guide to new concept
and production cars worldwide

MERRELL
LONDON · NEW YORK

# MERRELL

First published 2003 by Merrell Publishers Limited

**Head office**
42 Southwark Street
London SE1 1UN
Telephone +44 (0)20 7403 2047
E-mail mail@merrellpublishers.com

**New York office**
49 West 24th Street
New York, NY 10010
Telephone 212 929 8344
E-mail info@merrellpublishersusa.com

www.merrellpublishers.com

**Publisher** Hugh Merrell
**Editorial Director** Julian Honer
**US Director** Joan Brookbank
**Sales and Marketing Director** Emilie Nangle
**Managing Editor** Anthea Snow
**Editor** Sam Wythe
**Design Manager** Kate Ward
**Production Manager** Michelle Draycott
**Editorial and Production Assistant** Emily Sanders

A catalog record for this book is available from the Library of Congress

ISBN 1 85894 196 2

Consultant editor: Giles Chapman
Edited by Richard Dawes with Laura Hicks and Chuck Brandstater
Designed by Kate Ward
Layout by Marit Münzberg
Printed and bound in Spain

Frontispiece: Jaguar XJ; pages 4–5: Saab 9-3;
pages 8–9: Subaru B11S Coupé; pages 18–19: Porsche Cayenne

# Contents

# Trends, Highlights, Predictions

Since *The Car Design Yearbook* was first published, in September 2002, many of the models it featured as concepts have gone into mass production, and a good deal more are nearing their retail debut. In *The Car Design Yearbook 2* we examine all the new production and concept cars unveiled in the intervening twelve months. It's quite a range, from commercially important replacements for established bestsellers up (or down, depending on your viewpoint) to exotic sports cars and wacky showpieces.

The book's intrinsic value is that it is published annually. As you collect each edition it builds into a uniquely comprehensive record that charts automotive design development. In a few years you can look back at how global car design has evolved and see which new ideas have become commonplace.

Once again we profile some important car designers: the work of J. Mays of Ford, Patrick le Quément of Renault, and Chris Bangle of BMW is chronicled and analyzed. And, in addition, we've provided two special feature sections that will interest the car-design enthusiast and professional: the first is about the objective of concept cars, the second covers the current trend for super-luxury cars. You'll find both of these at the back of the book.

There has been one seismic change in the car industry over the past twelve months. The death of Giovanni Agnelli, head of the Fiat Group, in January 2003 came just as a storm was breaking over the future of the Italian empire started by his grandfather in 1899. The continuing slump in Fiat sales in a viciously competitive market, and the contracted option of selling out to General Motors in 2004, caused a battle in Italy between the government, the Agnelli family, and the banks that have propped up Fiat for several years. As Fiat is custodian of the Lancia, Alfa Romeo, Ferrari, and Maserati makes, there are rich pickings here for foreign car companies looking for a sporty presence in Europe. Already the vultures are circling. Any breakup of Fiat's embattled empire could see these makes fall into foreign hands—an embarrassing and frustrating scenario for the Italian government.

Designers in the car industry shift from continent to continent, adapting their skills to specific makes and markets. Still, there are very visible differences between the major car-design communities in

The new Honda Accord is just as inoffensive as its predecessor and yet is set to become another bestseller for the Japanese car giant.

Europe, America, and Japan. Even minimally informed observers can probably guess where a car is likely to have been designed just by looking at it; but to describe what it is about its "DNA" that denotes that visual origin is more challenging.

The USA has a long tradition of building large cars and trucks that usually require large-capacity engines to power them. In the country that has the world's biggest domestic market, and also some of the tightest speed and environmental restrictions anywhere, these have taken a different evolutionary path from cars in other parts of the world.

From a European or Japanese viewpoint, many American cars lack design subtlety. Then again, to look bold from every angle is perceived as a plus by the US auto executives, who need to keep their products selling. And, don't forget, Detroit has an enviable record as a trend-setting styling innovator, from the Chrysler Airflow and Lincoln Zephyr in the 1930s through the 1950s Studebakers, the 1960 Chevrolet Corvair, 1964 Ford Mustang, 1967 Oldsmobile Toronado, and 1983 Chrysler Voyager to the "cab-forward" stance pioneered by Chrysler sedans in the early 1990s.

Nonetheless, the grilles on American cars continue to be not just striking but also often very dominating. Strong chrome slats are used to emphasize the width, height, or power of the car—often all three. As a design starting point this then necessitates dramatic surfaces, which can sometimes make American cars appear overbearing. Surface geometry and lines are not always harmonious, the focus being on large, powerful-looking wheels or an overall impression of toughness and protection. American car design sees no need to shrink from giving people what they want.

At the other end of the scale, Japanese-designed cars conform to a less striking proportion and design language—they seek never to offend. Most Japanese cars are aimed at buyers concerned principally with value and reliability, rather than a look-at-me design statement. This emphasis tends to be expressed in boxy proportions with an athletic flavor, straight feature lines, and tight surfaces.

The Japanese have realized there is huge market share to be had with these more mundane-looking models, pitched at buyers who regard cars as consumer durables and not socioeconomic iconography. The best example is the archly conventional Honda Accord. Eight million have been sold worldwide since its first, modest appearance in 1976. This is not to say Honda uses dumb design. Quite the contrary: it designs cars that will sell to the masses and ensure long-term success in business.

European manufacturers sometimes take a more intellectual approach to design, and there are interesting differences—noticeable, country-specific design traits—between the member countries. Italy possesses emotive brands like Ferrari and Alfa Romeo that use carefully crafted and sporty lines to generate emotion and excitement at the very first glance. The subtlety of these surfaces and lines has been refined over decades by Fiat and Italian design houses like Pininfarina, Bertone, and Italdesign—companies that really progress car design and strive to bring new models to market. Recent examples that break the mold include the Fiat Multipla, the Alfa Romeo 147, and a whole raft of brilliant concept cars. How successful Fiat would have become if its Italian-inspired designs had been matched by Japanese standards of engineering quality is worth pondering.

In Germany, the combination of sportiness and conservatism is a constant theme. Volkswagen dominates the market with the hugely practical Golf—well built, square, and solid-looking. Other brands, such as BMW, have perfected their DNA over the decades, an evolution that has created the ultimate in sporty drivers' cars, while Porsche has built itself up through success in motorsport. Teutonic interiors and absolute functionality take preference over emotional aesthetics, resulting in an engineered look. The new Porsche Cayenne struggles to combine its SUV proportions with Porsche's sports-car design DNA, but owing to its functionality, build quality, and brand strength this car is guaranteed to be a big success.

In France, outstanding design from Renault, Peugeot, and Citroën challenges rival manufacturers around the world with arresting shapes and clever concepts, happily proving that even in this time of overcapacity it's possible to make a profit without being a multinational company. The Renault–Nissan alliance is fascinating. As economies of scale kick in and a new Nissan corporate image is carried through to the whole range, this partnership will be a great force in Europe. The C-Airdream concept from Citroën and the new Renault Espace demonstrate that the French approach interior design

**Opposite and above**
Many car manufacturers are trying to exploit new vehicle niches to capitalize on the heavy overall investments they need to make. The new Cayenne from Porsche, the result of a joint venture with Volkswagen, is one example that also has the advantage of carrying an extremely strong brand badge.

**Left**
Renault's strong commitment to design sees the new
Espace monospace sculpted into a model that is more
evocative than the previous incarnation.

**Opposite**
Few concepts ever break the mould like Citroën's
dramatic C-Airdream. Beautiful flowing lines and a
completely glazed roof make this car appear to offer
a totally new driving experience.

differently from the Germans; they normally choose warm, inviting colors for their interiors, in stark contrast to the somber, darker colors typical of German cars.

British makes, such as Jaguar and Aston Martin, have recently launched new products too. As with most British design, respect for heritage is a key value, and these latest models don't stray far from their predecessors' classic proportions and design values. London is increasingly important in "holistic" automotive design research, as evidenced by the recent opening of Ford's Ingeni complex and Nissan's design studio. Both look at trends in design and take inspiration from contemporary art, architecture, fashion, and design in what is perhaps Europe's most cosmopolitan and design-conscious city.

At Volvo, design director Peter Horbury has been appointed executive director of design for the whole of Ford's Premier Automotive Group, of which Volvo is a major part. He is now responsible for overseeing future product-design strategy and design processes for Aston Martin, Jaguar, Land Rover, and Volvo. This change reinforces the importance design plays within PAG, although Horbury's well-honed "Swedishness," as evinced in the S80 and XC90, with their "strong" shoulders, reassuring width, and chiseled details, is unlikely to filter into the British trio under his aegis.

There is, however, a dire warning to car designers when it comes to national characteristics. Sometimes a critical success is not a commercial one. You can deride the "very American" Ford F-150 pickup for its lack of finesse, but the customers love it. The "very Italian" Fiat Multipla, on the other hand, pushes the boundaries for mini-MPVs but has divided consumer opinion, and, in doing so, halved the number of potential buyers. So which is, in truth, the better design? It's a tough call.

Another area of development for most manufacturers over the past year has been the drive to extract more niche vehicles from existing brands. This creates more interest in new market niches and attracts new customers. And it's not just a matter of typical niche cars, like estates, convertibles, and SUVs, but sometimes more subtle blends of existing products, created to meet the needs of modern consumers. Or—even better—to offer them a product they didn't know they wanted until they saw it. Examples are

Porsche, with its new Cayenne, capitalizing on a strong, sporty brand image and a seemingly always-expanding market sector; Aston Martin's AMV8 Vantage, bringing the famous badge within reach of Porsche and Mercedes AMG customers; and Toyota's Scion make, launched initially in California, taking existing Toyota cars from Japan and rebranding them with small changes. Scion attempts to target the youth market, with the aim of getting Toyota group products into the hands of consumers at an early age and then keeping them there throughout their car-buying lives.

The BMW xActivity is a lifestyle vehicle that combines SUV flexibility with the roofless fun of a convertible. MCC, which brought us the nifty little Smart City Coupé, has recently launched its new coupé-roadster. Based on a simple design construction, low cost, and specially lightweight materials, this image-conscious model will appeal to those who want contemporary open-top fun but can't afford the more powerful Toyota MR2 or Lotus Elise.

In terms of production models, highlights of the past year include the new Z4 from BMW, a much more masculine replacement for the Z3, which uses BMW's new "flame surfacing" design language. Also new is the long-awaited Ford Streetka, the convertible sister model to Ford's popular A-segment Ka. Ford missed an opportunity by not launching it several years ago, but it will certainly reignite interest in the Ka brand and draw new people into Ford showrooms.

The new Mégane from Renault is particularly exciting in its proportional makeup. The stepped-out trunk may take some getting used to, but those excited by new car designs should seriously consider this model. Only sales success of the current range of new Renault cars will quicken the pace of concept innovation. Companies like Renault are best equipped to generate new ideas, so it would be a great pity if consumers weren't bold enough to buy into them. Meanwhile the Touareg is a key new model for Volkswagen, helping it push the brand upmarket toward more lucrative sales arenas, and in a segment that is still trendy and growing. This new SUV is an obvious choice for Volkswagen customers who want a bigger car and something more fashionable without having to desert the brand they trust.

And, of course, we cannot overlook Rolls-Royce and its newly launched Phantom. The Phantom is the result of unprecedented investment from new owner BMW. The press—tabloid, business, and specialist motoring—will eagerly monitor its success or failure, and any collapse of the US or European economies could spell disaster for a car that is a totally non-essential, luxury indulgence. Traditional customers may balk at Rolls-Royce's new German ownership, and the fact that most components are sourced from Germany, and then there is competition as never before from other new super-luxury models that may wreck BMW's sales projections.

From a concept standpoint, there is much to celebrate over the past year. Gorgeous sports cars like the elegant C-Airdream show the amount of thought and design skill that go into producing the very best concept cars. The Renault Ellypse again demonstrates the intellectual approach the company adopts for proportions, surface language, features, colors, and textures. As a result, Renault creates concepts worthy of major design exhibitions and brings new interior and exterior thoughts into the world for everyone to debate.

The Aston Martin AMV8 Vantage is a dream come true for anyone wishing to spend $100,000 on a sports car who might otherwise have had to make the conventional choice and go for a rather plebeian Porsche Carrera. Designed by Henrik Fisker, the AMV8 Vantage is based on the Vanquish's aluminum platform and has all the hallmarks of a model that will transform Aston Martin sales.

Sometimes concept cars are a way of overtly showing a new direction for a brand. The Cadillac Sixteen concept is one; it's hard to see how this can be anything but a pure marketing tool. With sixteen cylinders and a length of nearly 5.7 meters (18.7 ft), the Sixteen is absolutely massive. In revealing it, General Motors clearly says that it, too, can produce models for the super-luxury market. But Cadillac will surely study the business case very thoroughly before committing to such an expensive project, especially in a crowded sector with small investment returns. This is all about corporate egos.

The Ford Mustang, on the other hand, is an American institution. The latest concept was well received at the North American International Auto Show in Detroit in 2003, and the production version is now eagerly awaited.

In a surprise move at the Detroit show, the Mini Cooper was named North American Car of the Year. It was singled out for its sporty handling and performance, superb design, practicality, and affordability. The Mini Cooper is the first British-built car ever to win the award, judged by a panel of American motoring journalists, Whether this can be taken as a sign that there is a desire for much smaller cars in America is unclear—low US fuel prices would appear to militate against that.

So what does the near-term future hold? We can expect an explosion of niche vehicles, with manufacturers trying to capitalize on huge tooling and infrastructure investments, so we'll see more convertibles, estates, crossovers, and mini-MPVs. This approach is regarded as an excellent way of getting potential customers to buy into a make, and, once brand-loyal, they'll keep spending on it throughout the different stages of their car-owning lifetimes.

Other innovations will likely include more combinations of crossover capability in all types of car. Flexible interiors that allow load-carrying capability one minute and office functionality the next will come to be expected as the norm, not as a costly indulgence.

Modern interpretations of retro design have proved successful; the Mini and the Chrysler PT Cruiser are good examples. This indicates that people want striking design iterated in a high-quality way. But in 2003–4 we're in a phase of car design where the current language uses strong architectural surfaces, strong feature lines, and yet conservative themes. "Chiseled" design is another way to put it—a movement that leaves the emotional, friendly curves behind. This trend is sure to continue apace, but the buying public will decide whether it wants it or not. If it doesn't, we'll probably see softer and friendlier designs coming through.

Exteriors have improved greatly over the past decade; with developments in plastics technology and lamp design, a car's whole exterior can now fit together tightly to give excellent wind-noise suppression and aerodynamic performance. Interior design, by contrast, has much more scope now for radical change. Ford's Lincoln division, for example, is investing three times as much in interior design as in exteriors.

America's bestselling truck is once again updated. This time the Ford F-150 comes with much greater emphasis on both refinement and comfort, but the ruggedness in its exterior design clearly remains undiminished.

A–Z of New Models

# Acura TSX

| Design | Honda Motor Corporation |
|---|---|
| Engine | 2.4 in-line 4 |
| Power | 149 kW (200 bhp) @ 6800 rpm |
| Torque | 225 Nm (166 lb. ft) @ 4500 rpm |
| Gearbox | 6-speed manual |
| Front suspension | Double wishbone |
| Rear suspension | Multi-link |
| Brakes front/rear | Discs/discs |
| Front tires | P215/50R17 |
| Rear tires | P215/50R17 |
| Length | 4657 mm (183.3 in.) |
| Width | 1762 mm (69.4 in.) |
| Height | 1456 mm (57.3 in.) |
| Fuel consumption | 9.4 ltr/100 km (20.8 mpg) |

The all-new Acura TSX sports sedan went on sale in the US during the spring of 2003. This new model, with its sharply wedged design, is aimed directly at grabbing market share from European competitors, such as BMW's 3-series and Volvo's S60.

The TSX will sit in Acura's line-up between the RSX sports coupé and Acura's top-selling model, the 3.2 TL executive sedan.

With a distinctive V-shaped grille and trapezoidal headlights, the look is characterful and sporty. In fact, the silhouette, together with some of the feature lines, could have been lifted straight from the Alfa Romeo 156, a car that has enjoyed great success in Europe among design-conscious buyers. Significantly, the 156 has also eaten into BMW territory.

At the back, the wide C-pillars wrap around to a rear screen that falls down to the short trunk lid, in that sporty, typically BMW 3-Series way. The trunk drops away vertically, past the narrow rear lights and on to a simple rear bumper that houses twin chrome tailpipes.

The cockpit matches the outside in its sportiness, and also uses good-quality materials. However, the combination of perforated leather on the sports seats with black leather, wood, and aluminum detailing gives a look that is now overused and tired; the aluminum, in particular, is stark among the other, softer shades.

Although the instruments are clearly visible through the sporty, three-spoke steering wheel, the interior doesn't have the emotional flair of the exterior, even though it's obviously well appointed. Few marks here, then, for design innovation.

# Alfa Romeo Kamal

| Engine | 3.2 V6 |
|---|---|
| Power | 186 kW (250 bhp) @ 6200 rpm |
| Torque | 300 Nm (221 lb. ft) @ 4800 rpm |
| Gearbox | 6-speed manual |
| Installation | Front-engined/all-wheel drive |
| Height | 1620 mm (63.8 in.) |

At the Geneva Motor Show in 2003, Alfa Romeo showed the Kamal, designed at the Arese Style Center in Italy. Not a working car, this is an exterior model of an envisaged Alfa SUV, with a design strongly linked to the production 147, but with more voluptuous surfaces and a more purposeful stance. The SUV niche is one that most other manufacturers have been attacking with gusto of late.

The name "Kamal" comes from the ancient Sanskrit language, where it means "red," a color long associated with the Alfa Romeo insignia. In Arabic the same word means "perfection", or the "synthesis of opposites." All these epithets are fine as associations, the Fiat-controlled brand has decided, and indeed anything that can boost the appeal of Fiat-made products right now is welcome, no matter how at odds it is with company tradition, for the fact is, Alfa Romeo has never built an SUV before.

The front is in traditional Alfa Romeo style, with the design lines all drawing the eye to the point of the center grille. The strong openings either side of the grille, reminiscent of those of the BMW Z8, give a very powerful, sporty impression. The bulges in the wheel arches are highlighted by the sinuous waistline, which droops over the front door before rising up to finish at the rear light.

A car like this could achieve good sales in the current market, and an Alfa Romeo would make an intriguing alternative to the mainly German, Japanese, and British options on offer in Europe. The model could share many components with the 147 and 156, but Alfa's typical fragility—fine in sports and racing cars but no good if you're stuck in the middle of nowhere—needs to be banished if massive warranty claims are not to be an unhappy by-product of selling a real-life Kamal.

# Aston Martin AMV8 Vantage

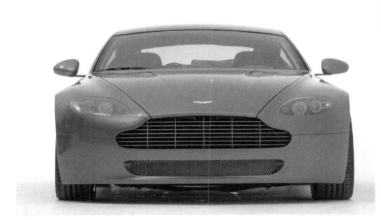

An impressive new model to be launched by Aston Martin in 2005 is seen here in concept form as the AMV8 Vantage. It's intended as a new, small Aston Martin that will compete directly with Porsche—a size of car not made by the British company since the DB2 series back in the 1950s. In addition, this aims to boost Aston Martin's production significantly, and it could turn out to be the most important launch in the company's eighty-nine-year history.

The name Vantage has historic links with Aston Martin; it first appeared on the DB2 in 1950 to denote a high-performance engine option. This time, though, it's used to identify a specific model name. The AMV8 Vantage is a two-seater sports car retaining a front-engined/rear-wheel-drive layout for 50:50 weight distribution. Much of the car's structure will evolve from the top-end Vanquish, which features aluminum and composites. According to Aston Martin, the exterior design is 90% true to the production version, but the interior will be reworked for 2005.

Traditional Aston Martin design cues have been used, including the front grille shape and the side air-intake strakes, as found on all Aston Martins. The AMV8 Vantage is, however, a thoroughly modern interpretation of the company's heritage.

Inside, the designers have—sensibly—specified everything you see and touch as uniquely Aston Martin and not taken from a Ford parts bin. After all, if TVR can do that at half the price, then Aston Martin customers should expect it too.

The interior is finished in an imaginative combination of different leathers and anodized aluminum. Customers will be offered a huge choice of upholstery schemes and the option of different materials on request. A wide range of body colors will also be available.

Even though production numbers will be higher than for existing models such as the DB7, the car should still be pretty exclusive. And that is one characteristic of the British brand that can't be altered too radically.

| Design | Henrik Fisker |
|---|---|
| Engine | 4.3 V8 |
| Installation | Front mid-engined/rear-wheel drive |
| Brakes front/rear | Discs/discs |
| Length | 4347 mm (171.1 in.) |
| Width | 1874 mm (73.8 in.) |
| Height | 1298 mm (51.1 in.) |
| Wheelbase | 2600 mm (102.4 in.) |
| Curb weight | 1500 kg (3307 lb.) |

Aston Martin AMV8 Vantage **27**

# Audi A3

| | |
|---|---|
| Design | Peter Schreyer |
| Engine | 3.2 V6 (2.0 and 2.0 diesel in-line 4 also offered) |
| Torque | 320 Nm (236 lb. ft) |
| Gearbox | 6-speed manual |
| Installation | Front-engined/all-wheel drive |
| Front suspension | MacPherson strut |
| Rear suspension | 4-link |
| Length | 4203 mm (165.5 in.) |
| Width | 1765 mm (69.5 in.) |
| Height | 1421 mm (55.9 in.) |
| Wheelbase | 2578 mm (101.5 in.) |
| Curb weight | 1348 kg (2972 lb.) |

Since its launch in 1996, the Audi A3 has achieved fantastic sales in the premium-hatchback segment by combining a high-quality product with conservative and safe design that appeals strongly to the middle-class market. A bit "square," some might think, though others would say stylishly timeless.

The new model is identical in its approach—obviously a sensible move, as it would be foolish to scare off a loyal customer base. But there are some changes. In fact, probably the best way to describe the new look is that it has been sharpened up, and as a result the new A3 is slightly sportier than its predecessor. At the front, the headlights are now clear, with technical-looking reflectors inside them. There are crisper lines in the hood and the front bumper now has sharp, vented air intakes with small radii. Along the side there's now a sharp, rising feature line that extends through the gas-tank flap to the rear lights. The rear is constructed mainly of horizontal and vertical lines, and is slightly less curvaceous than in the previous model.

Interior space has been improved, thanks to an increase of 65 mm (2.6 in.) in the wheelbase. The sober interior design is very similar to what was offered last time, made up of taut lines and featuring materials in dark and light gray.

The new, sharper A3 went on sale during the summer of 2003 and is surely destined to continue the success for Audi in this small sector, one that it helped shape and now utterly dominates. It must be thankful it possesses a design that can mature so assuredly.

# Audi A8

| Engine | 4.2 V8 (3.7 V8 also offered) |
|---|---|
| Power | 246 kW (330 bhp) @ 6500 rpm |
| Torque | 430 Nm (317 lb. ft) @ 3500 rpm |
| Gearbox | 6-speed Tiptronic |
| Installation | Front-engined/all-wheel drive |
| Front suspension | Double-wishbone air suspension |
| Rear suspension | Trapezoidal-link axle with air suspension |
| Brakes front/rear | Discs/discs, ESP, ABS, EBD, BA |
| Front tires | 235/55R17 |
| Rear tires | 235/55R17 |
| Length | 5051 mm (198.9 in.) |
| Width | 1894 mm (74.6 in.) |
| Height | 1444 mm (56.9 in.) |
| Wheelbase | 2944 mm (115.9 in.) |
| Track front/rear | 1629/1615 mm (64.1/63.6 in.) |
| Curb weight | 1780 kg (3924 lb.) |
| 0–100 km/h (62 mph) | 6.3 sec |
| Top speed | 250 km/h (155 mph) governed |
| Fuel consumption | 12 ltr/100 km (19.6 mpg) |
| $CO_2$ emissions | 287 g/km |

The new A8 is the brand flagship model for Audi. This is a model that is renowned for pioneering new technology: the first A8, introduced in 1994 to replace the slow-selling and rather anonymous Audi V8, was the first luxury car to use aluminum for both frame and body; indeed, it was the first all-aluminum car to go into volume production. This is a weight-saving and environmentally friendly route to executive car-making that has been emulated by Jaguar with its new XJ.

Although the exterior is subtly different from that of the old model, particularly at the rear, the new internal technology is the most interesting aspect of the new A8. The aluminum body is based on a further development of the Audi Space Frame (ASF); Audi claims it is stiffer and more refined.

For the chassis, adaptive air suspension with continuously adjustable damping gives an optimum balance between comfort and handling, depending on the driving mode selected. The driver can choose from one of four pre-defined settings: an automatic mode, where the body is at the standard height but lowered by 25 mm (1 in.) if the car is driven at more than 120 km/h (75 mph); a dynamic mode, where the car is lowered by 20 mm (0.8 in.) before it sets off, and the air suspension operates with firmer springs and a harder damping characteristic; a comfort mode, to help the car glide smoothly over bumpy surfaces; and a "lift" mode, designed for driving on uneven terrain, which can be activated below 80 km/h (50 mph) to raise ground clearance by 25 mm, with the balanced damping characteristics of the automatic mode.

Other electronic systems fitted include the electromechanical parking brake and the radar-assisted distance control system known as "adaptive cruise control."

The original A8 was regarded as an all-round high performer, albeit one with a less defined character than its rivals. But this new model promises a lot more, and will surely bite much harder into the sales of the new BMW 7 Series.

# Audi Nuvolari

| | |
|---|---|
| Design | Walter De Silva |
| Engine | 5.0 V10 bi-turbo |
| Power | 447 kW (600 bhp) |
| Torque | 750 Nm (553 lb. ft) @ 2000 rpm |
| Installation | Front-engined/all-wheel drive |
| Front suspension | 4-link |
| Rear suspension | Trapezoidal link |
| Brakes front/rear | Discs/discs |
| Front tires | 265/720 R 560 PAX |
| Rear tires | 265/720 R 560 PAX |
| Length | 4800 mm (188.9 in.) |
| Width | 1920 mm (75.6 in.) |
| Height | 1410 mm (55.5 in.) |
| 0–100 km/h (62 mph) | 4.1 sec |
| Top speed | 250 km/h (155 mph) |

The Audi Nuvolari design study is named after the motor-racing driver Tazio Nuvolari, the last man to win a grand prix in an Auto Union car, in Belgrade in 1939. Nuvolari died in 1953, but is still famous for his daring, spectacular driving style and the yellow pullover he always wore at the wheel.

This quattro concept study is a vision for a powerful Gran Turismo car, a two-door two-plus-two coupé with GT proportions. Its design lines are superficially similar to those of the Audi TT, but this GT has much more presence.

The long hood, the high waistline, and the arched roofline that drops smoothly at the rear dominate its silhouette; the high waistline makes the windows extremely shallow, as in the Audi TT. At the side, though, is a dynamic line in the sill, and higher up is a feature line that clips the edge of the bulging wheel arches housing the massive wheels, which are set with minimum overhang.

Some new technology is featured. The LED headlights have allowed the designers more freedom because they need less installation space than conventional ones. For enhanced personal protection, two cameras check for occupant position in the event that the airbag needs to be inflated. For security, the glove compartment is opened by fingerprint recognition—cute, if a little paranoid.

Inside the car, leather and aluminum materials are combined: contrasting Stromboli black and Carrara white for the leather, while cool aluminum adds design structure to the dashboard, doors, and center console, all designed to encapsulate GT philosophy.

Audi claims the Nuvolari outlines the future direction for the brand. If this is true, it's an extremely exciting proposition.

# Audi Pikes Peak

| Design | Walter De Silva |
|---|---|
| Engine | 4.2 V8 |
| Power | 373 kW (500 bhp) |
| Installation | Front-engined/4-wheel drive |
| Brakes front/rear | Discs/discs |
| 0–100 km/h (62 mph) | 4.9 sec |

Not wanting to be left behind by the SUV bandwagon, Audi has designed this quattro. The Pikes Peak combines massive power with all-terrain capability and MPV versatility. The name comes from the Pike's Peak hill-climb race held in Colorado, USA, every June—an event Audi has won three times.

Externally, the Pikes Peak is an up-to-the-minute interpretation of the Audi Allroad but with dedicated off-road capability and more power. Technical details on the exterior include loop-pattern door handles that extend when proximity sensors detect the key-holder is approaching. The handles are also illuminated, and lights in the exterior mirrors illuminate the area around the doors. The body is set off by huge, five-arm, double-spoke wheels.

The interior is also innovative. A four-plus-two configuration allows the Pikes Peak to be adapted from sports car to off-roader to people-carrier. Off-road competence comes from the car's variable-height adaptive air suspension and four-wheel-drive drivetrain. The ride height can be raised for rough terrain but is automatically lowered when the car is back on smooth roads. A glass roof provides plenty of light to the interior, where leather-upholstered seats accommodate up to six people. The interior also includes laser optics, a DVD entertainment system, and Internet access.

Audi says that while there are currently no plans to put the Pikes Peak into full production, it will study public opinion very closely. Manufacturers always say that. Still, the car would do extremely well in the current market despite a plethora of existing and upcoming competitors.

SWADA 01

# Bentley Continental GT

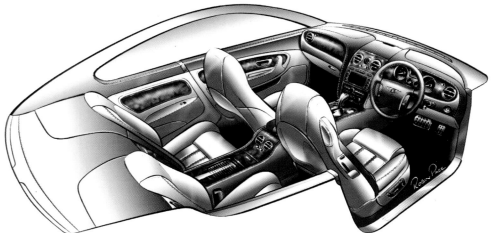

Now under the ownership of the VW Group, Bentley finds itself for the first time since the 1950s (and the genesis of the original R-type Continental) in the enviable position of being allowed to invest heavily in new products. Since 1965 all Bentleys have been based on derivatives and descendants of the Rolls-Royce Silver Shadow platform, and this has hampered handling, performance, and general sportiness. The new Continental GT changes all that, and received great acclaim at the 2002 Paris Motor Show.

This long-anticipated new model is based on the Volkswagen Phaeton platform, which also underpins the new Audi A8. It is fitted with a Bentley-developed version of Volkswagen's W12 engine, a massively powerful and smooth unit that is key to the Continental's performance promise. This new sports coupé is not just the fastest model in Bentley's illustrious eighty-three-year history: it also happens to be the fastest four-seater coupé in the world.

The design philosophy behind the Continental GT was to produce a vehicle with true supercar performance that carries four people and their luggage and displays the highest levels of refinement. References are made to the 1950s R-type Continental—in particular the "suggested" front and rear wings, the gently tapering fastback, and the interplay between the side window shape and the tautly gathered waistline. Yet much of the design "formality" of recent Bentleys has been discarded: obtrusive, "separate" bumpers are gone; the Bentley grille is a stylized shadow of its former gaunt self; and the seamless, harmonious integration of body panels has an unmistakable aura of current Audi styling.

Inside, the cabin remains true to the make's values, with chrome, fine woods, and leather that adorn the space as in almost every Bentley of the past. The instrument panel now splits at the center console to distinguish the driver's space from the front passenger's. The British veneer remains, but the Continental GT is vastly more contemporary European in its interior lines.

Crusty Bentley traditionalists will need time to adjust, but, crucially, the new model catapults Bentley into the twenty-first century and is a brand-new basis from which other derivatives can be explored.

# Bertone Birusa

The Bertone Birusa is one of the most fascinating concept cars in this book. Based on the BMW Z8, this high-performance GT car is equipped with a 298-kW (400-bhp) engine and dramatic gullwing doors. Like the design, the name is striking: it's derived from the adjective "biross," which in Piedmontese dialect describes a brilliant, resourceful person.

The Birusa has a classic two-box configuration, dominated by the imposing slope of the extremely long hood and the teardrop-shaped cabin, which tapers toward the rear end, pushing the occupants well toward the rear axle. The massive 51-cm (20-in.) wheels and the unique side-window line, which drops at the front to give the low-seated driver better vision, dominate the side view. These thin, rectangular proportions are echoed in other features, such as the headlights, the hood vents, and the slender rear LED lights. The surface form of the Birusa is quite gentle; it's the shape and the proportions of the constituent elements that give it such an amazing presence. Two cameras have replaced rear-view mirrors and the rear window is actually a sunroof made of heat-resistant glass.

Other innovations include the power-assisted gullwing doors made from carbon fiber. These are voice-activated, like the sunroof, the semi-adaptive headlights, and an infrared nighttime vision system.

Bertone has created a car of extreme proportions, and we wonder if BMW will be tempted to use these in future models. If you get a chance to see this car "in the flesh," then take it—it's the only way you'll fully appreciate it.

| Design | Bertone |
| --- | --- |
| Engine | 5.0 V8 |
| Power | 298 kW (400 bhp) @ 6600 rpm |
| Gearbox | 6-speed manual |
| Installation | Front-engined/rear-wheel drive |
| Brakes front/rear | Discs/discs |
| Front tires | 255/35R20 |
| Rear tires | 275/35R20 |
| Length | 4400 mm (173.2 in.) |
| Width | 1900 mm (74.8 in.) |
| Wheelbase | 2850 mm (112.2 in.) |

# BMW xActivity

| | |
|---|---|
| Design | Chris Bangle |
| Engine | 3.0 in-line 6 |
| Power | 172 kW (231 bhp) |
| Gearbox | 5-speed manual/4-wheel drive |
| Installation | Front-engined/all-wheel drive |
| Brakes front/rear | Discs/discs |
| Front tires | 245/45R18 |
| Rear tires | 275/40R18 |
| Length | 4550 mm (179.1 in.) |
| Width | 1800 mm (70.9 in.) |
| Height | 1660 mm (65.4 in.) |
| Wheelbase | 2790 mm (109.8 in.) |

BMW has enjoyed great success across the globe with its X5 SUV. Now it's investigating how to capitalize on this by offering another "X" model, the xActivity, a so-called Sports Activity Vehicle (SAV) with a combination of dynamic looks and on- and off-road driving characteristics.

Although the xActivity is still just a concept, its proportions are clearly linked to those of the X5, and individual features give a preview of what a future BMW SAV may resemble.

The exterior design uses characteristic alternating concave and convex surfaces, and a double-kidney grille married to a distinctive front end that has strong graphics between the lights. A strong but muted band also appears around the side windows, giving a modern touch. The proportions are typical of BMW, with a long wheelbase, short overhangs, and conspicuously flared wheel arches. But the most visually impressive feature is the frame-structure convertible roof, which combines the open-air thrill of a convertible with the robust appearance and structure of an SAV. The frameless side windows add to the car's "outdoor" nature.

The materials used inside the xActivity are both hard-wearing and high-quality, with natural cowhide meeting neoprene for a distinct and stylish contrast. Internally, the most impressive technological feature is the "smart materials" used for the seats, eliminating the need for electric or manual seat adjustment. These newly developed pressure-sensitive materials allow adjustment solely by application of pressure to the seats themselves. But how resilient this innovation will prove in the face of abuse is debatable.

# BMW Z4

| Design | Chris Bangle |
|---|---|
| Engine | 3.0 in-line 6 (2.5 in-line 6 also offered) |
| Power | 170 kW (231 bhp) @ 5900 rpm |
| Torque | 300 Nm (221 lb. ft) @ 3500 rpm |
| Gearbox | 6-speed manual |
| Installation | Front-engined/rear-wheel drive |
| Front suspension | MacPherson strut |
| Brakes front/rear | Discs/discs |
| Front tires | 225/45R17 |
| Rear tires | 225/45R17 |
| Length | 4091 mm (161.1 in.) |
| Width | 1781 mm (70.1 in.) |
| Height | 1299 mm (51.1 in.) |
| Wheelbase | 2495 mm (98.2 in.) |
| Curb weight | 1290 kg (2844 lb.) |
| 0–100 km/h (62 mph) | 5.9 sec |
| Top speed | 250 km/h (155 mph) |
| Fuel consumption | 9.11 ltr/100 km (25.8 mpg) |
| CO$_2$ emissions | 221 g/km |

The BMW Z4 roadster replaces the Z3, the American-built two-seater sports car launched in 1995 that was widely lambasted by motoring critics for its design and lackluster performance. This panning, though, was no bar to popularity among buyers whose main criteria were style, prestige, and ease of ownership, and now BMW's design chief, Chris Bangle, has righted the entry-level roadster and endowed it with a much purer sports appeal.

Based closely on the style of the CS1 concept car shown at Geneva in 2002, the Z4 dispenses with the two rear seats to give a dedicated two-seater layout, and also makes a number of refinements to the exterior surfaces. Gone is the horizontal waistline in favor of a slightly more curvaceous side profile. Added is the wing crease that strikes through a large BMW badge in front of the doors, and the trunk lid now has a moulded-in spoiler complete with centrally high-mounted stoplight (the industry abbreviation is CHMSL!) The new Z4 is much more coherent in its design as a muscular car. By comparison, the Z3 had a rather "masculine" front yet a "feminine" tail treatment.

The Z4's interior enjoys classic roadster design that is straightforward, clear, modern, and elegant, with black and silver as the main color finishes. The instrument panel is curved toward the inside; the center console is shaped like a letter "T" facing toward the instrument panel. Conventionally in a sports car, the speedometer and rev counter dominate the dashboard, with tube-like covers to protect them against distracting light reflection from the windshield.

The complex exterior surfaces of this car generate unique shadows, depending on the light and the angle from which you view it. Chris Bangle can only be commended for bringing the Z4 to production reality. It looks great, and is no doubt the perfect machine for a weekend jaunt on country lanes.

# Buick Centieme

| | |
|---|---|
| Design | Gary Mack |
| Engine | 3.6 V6 twin-turbo |
| Power | 298 kW (400 bhp) |
| Torque | 543 Nm (400 lb. ft) |
| Gearbox | 4-speed automatic |
| Installation | Front-engined/all-wheel drive |
| Front suspension | MacPherson strut |
| Rear suspension | Short and long arm |
| Brakes front/rear | Discs/discs |
| Front tires | P275/40R22 |
| Rear tires | P275/40R22 |
| Length | 4786 mm (188.4 in.) |
| Width | 1971 mm (77.6 in.) |
| Height | 1634 mm (64.3 in.) |
| Wheelbase | 3026 mm (119.1 in.) |
| Track front/rear | 1697/1709 mm (66.8/67.3 in.) |
| Curb weight | 1792 kg (3951 lb.) |

Buick launched the Centieme to commemorate its one-hundredth anniversary. The Italian design consultant Bertone built this concept, a luxurious vehicle combining the features of a sedan with those of a typical SUV.

The Centieme seats six in rows of two. It has a low, wide stance and sports flowing surfaces that are perhaps too curvaceous, feature lines, and a classic, if dominating, Buick grille. Combined with a relatively long wheelbase, tight overhangs, and a rising daylight opening line, these features give the car a nimble and energetic appearance.

Inside, the luxury is evident, with no expense spared. The seating for the first two rows uses captain's chairs. Armrests are located on the adjacent doors and integrated in the seats for symmetry and greater comfort. Porcelain-colored leather covers the seats and the lower doors. Dusk-colored leather on the third-row seating and upper doors contrasts beautifully with the lighter hue of the first and second rows, giving the cabin a beguiling ambience.

Porcelain soft-touch suede is used for the headlining, while the leather floor is custom-made and hints at highly contemporary home decor. The steering wheel, consoles, and interior trim are accented in olive ash, and the cluster gauges have aluminum detailing.

The Centieme is designed to celebrate a century of Buick heritage while harnessing contemporary values. Sleek, romantic lines accentuate full, sculptural forms to create what might well be the future for Buick designs. But remember: this is a show car, pure and simple.

# Cadillac Sixteen

| | |
|---|---|
| Design | Wayne Cherry |
| Engine | 13.6 V16 |
| Power | 746 kW (1000 bhp) @ 6000 rpm |
| Torque | 1357 Nm (1000 lb. ft) @ 4300 rpm |
| Gearbox | 4-speed automatic |
| Installation | Front-engined/rear-wheel drive |
| Front suspension | High-arm short and long arm |
| Rear suspension | Semi-trailing arm |
| Brakes front/rear | Discs/discs |
| Front tires | 265/40R24 |
| Rear tires | 265/40R24 |
| Length | 5673 mm (223.3 in.) |
| Width | 2029 mm (79.9 in.) |
| Height | 1392 mm (54.8 in.) |
| Wheelbase | 3556 mm (140 in.) |
| Track front/rear | 1766/1766 mm (69.5/69.5 in.) |
| Curb weight | 2270 kg (5005 lb.) |
| 0–100 km/h (62 mph) | 4 sec (est.) |
| Top speed | 322 km/h (200 mph) |
| Fuel consumption | 11.8 ltr/100 km (20 mpg) |

At almost 5.7 meters (18.7 ft) in length, and with 13.6 liters of V16 power, the new Cadillac Sixteen concept is all about a marketing vision for General Motors' premium Cadillac brand. These cars are seen as designs that embody solidness, power, and luxury in a new, modern way.

The Sixteen refers back to 1930, when Cadillac produced custom-built cars and the first V16 engine. This powered one of just three V16 production cars, and in 1932 Cadillac became the only carmaker ever to offer V8, V12, and V16 engines.

This concept displays grand, sculpted exterior proportions, with its sleek lines, very long wheelbase, and gigantic, 61-cm (24-in.) wheels. It's enormous in every respect. Wayne Cherry's team has used materials and techniques that draw on the coachbuilding traditions of the 1930s in areas such as upholstery, instrumentation, interior woodwork, and aluminum outer-body panels.

Outside, the Sixteen has a long aluminum hood, a dramatic grille, and vertical headlight clusters. The hugely raked screen lifts up on to an all-glass roof that sits without the support of the B-pillars. The C-pillars seem to drop endlessly, giving a pronounced, rearward-biased cabin proportion, yet the rear door glass drops acutely, making the C-pillars look strong and powerful, to match those vast wheels.

Power-operated hood panels that split along the center line, once more harking back to the 1930s, cover the engine compartment.

Inside are top-notch materials and opulent contemporary design: hand-stitched Tuscan leather upholstery for the seats, hand-woven silk carpets on the floor, and walnut-burl veneers on the dash, door panels, and console—and not forgetting the dashboard-mounted Bulgari clock.

The Sixteen concept is an extreme example of craftsmanship, but this is surely only a marketing exercise for the brand, to project a vision for the ultimate in Cadillac opulence. Unless GM really has been stung into action by Rolls-Royce and Maybach.

# Cadillac SRX

| | |
|---|---|
| Design | Kip Wasenko |
| Engine | 4.6 V8 |
| Power | 235 kW (315 bhp) @ 6400 rpm |
| Torque | 421 Nm (310 lb. ft) @ 4400 rpm |
| Gearbox | 5-speed automatic |
| Installation | Front-engined/rear-wheel drive |
| Front suspension | Short and long arm |
| Rear suspension | Multi-link |
| Brakes front/rear | Discs/discs |
| Front tires | P235/60R18 |
| Rear tires | P255/55R18 |
| Length | 4950 mm (194.9 in.) |
| Width | 1844 mm (72.6 in.) |
| Height | 1671 mm (65.8 in.) |
| Wheelbase | 2957 mm (116.4 in.) |
| Curb weight | 1948 kg (4295 lb.) |

The Cadillac SRX clearly reflects Cadillac's new design language, as evidenced in several concept cars over the past four years. These include the Evoq in 1999, the Imaj in 2000, the Vizon in 2001, and the Cien supercar in 2002. A shorthand definition of this design language would be: structural and boxy proportions, chiseled forms, and straight feature lines.

This approach endows the SRX with a tough-looking stance that will clearly make it stand out from the crowd of other, much softer SUVs—the Infiniti FX45 or the dramatic Mercedes-Benz GST (when it eventually arrives) spring to mind.

The SRX shares some design elements with the CTS production sedan, such as the V-shaped grille, and vertical tail lights and headlights—all features that appeared on Cadillacs back in 1965. The rear side glass and tailgate are visually disjointed along the waistline leading from the main seating area; this implies there is a separate area for luggage which offers more space than rival models do. Adequate ground clearance and dark-gray lower trim hint at off-road potential but without being too rugged.

Inside, there is an unfortunate lack of inspiration. Tedious gray and dark, polished wood mix with cream leather to create an interior design lacking the sumptuousness and tailored feel consumers expect in a top-end SUV. The instruments and switchgear are pleasingly straightforward, but, overall, the interior smacks of under-investment.

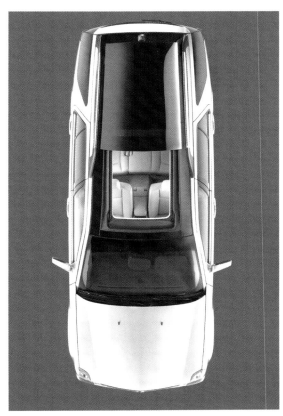

# Chevrolet Aveo

| | |
|---|---|
| Design | Italdesign |
| Engine | 1.6 in-line 4 |
| Power | 78 kW (105 bhp) @ 5800 rpm |
| Torque | 145 Nm (107 lb. ft) @ 3600 rpm |
| Gearbox | 5-speed manual |
| Installation | Front-engined/front-wheel drive |
| Front suspension | MacPherson strut |
| Rear suspension | Torsion beam |
| Brakes front/rear | Discs/drums |
| Front tires | P185/60R14 |
| Rear tires | P185/60R14 |
| Length | 4235 mm (166.7 in.) |
| Width | 1670 mm (65.7 in.) |
| Height | 1495 mm (58.9 in.) |
| Wheelbase | 2480 mm (97.6 in.) |
| Curb weight | 1080 kg (2381 lb.) |

Designed at Giorgetto Giugiaro's Italdesign studio in Turin, the new Aveo from Chevrolet comes as either a contemporary four-door sedan or a sporty five-door.

The five-door body style has a hood that rises steeply on to the arched roofline. A strong side feature starts at the headlights and grows into a wedge that runs through to the rear lights. Both the "drooping" feature in the lower half of the doors and the flared rear wheel arch add a little more visual interest to the side profile. Although the sedan has similar features, its door detailing is more horizontal, to reflect its greater length (the five-door model is 3800 mm/149.6 in. long).

Both cars are designed for mass-market appeal. They are totally inoffensive, mixing thoughtfully crafted proportions and attractive features to create models that are desirable for this marketplace but not too futuristic for the Chevrolet stable's sensible image. Points of interest include clear headlights with faceted lenses, jewel-like tail lights, and prominent gold Chevy "bowtie" badges front and rear.

Inside, the high roof and raised seats give good visibility and easy access, and are particularly welcome for their contribution to improving passive safety.

Chevrolet's marketers hope that launching the Aveo in the entry-level segment will allow the car to play an important role in luring new customers to the Chevy family. When it arrives at American dealers, some time in 2004, the Aveo will be positioned to compete with the bargain-basement Hyundai Accent and Kia Rio, and it, too, is to be built in Korea to keep costs down and ensure ultra-competitive pricing.

# Chevrolet Cheyenne

| Design | Jeff Angeleri |
|---|---|
| Engine | 6.0 V8 supercharged |
| Power | 373 kW (500 bhp) |
| Torque | 787 Nm (580 lb. ft) |
| Gearbox | 4-speed automatic |
| Installation | Front-engined/rear-wheel drive |
| Front suspension | Short and long arm |
| Rear suspension | IRS with rear steer |
| Brakes front/rear | Discs/discs |
| Front tires | 285/60R22 |
| Rear tires | 285/60R22 |
| Length | 5940 mm (233.9 in.) |
| Width | 2080 mm (81.9 in.) |
| Height | 1945 mm (76.6 in.) |
| Wheelbase | 3935 mm (154.9 in.) |
| Track front/rear | 1770/1770 mm (69.7/69.7 in.) |
| Curb weight | 2721 kg (1234 lb.) |

Chevrolet, which has been at the center of the pickup truck's evolution for decades, has long prided itself on its rugged image. But the new Cheyenne concept may be a sign of things to come: it has a softer, more elegant style, plus a greater cargo-carrying versatility thanks to its huge load bed.

Certain Chevy trucks of the past, most notably the 1955 Cameo, the 1967 and 1973 Cheyennes, and the 1988 Silverado, have made a great impression on General Motors' designers with their mix of design and function. The Cheyenne aims to capture the same iconic status.

Its cab is pushed further forward, allowing more interior space, and thus greater versatility and comfort, and the wheels are pushed further outward, giving the impression of increased stability. The two-panel glass roof with integrated sunroof and the wrap-around, "bubble back" rear glass accentuate the cab's openness.

The large cargo area could be quite tricky to reach, so Chevrolet has provided two side-access doors just behind the cab, as well as a traditional tailgate. There are multiple storage bins in the box floor, with lighting and integrated tie-downs for heavy jobs in all conditions.

Inside, the cab is simply surfaced and gives a sense of space. The instrument panel is low and uncluttered. Mottled saddle leather is used for the seats and headlining, while brushed satin-finish aluminum inlays in the doors and floor add a dash of quality.

This softened pickup attempts to inject some friendliness into a market that is crowded with tough, brutish-looking products. In doing so it may well find some new friends.

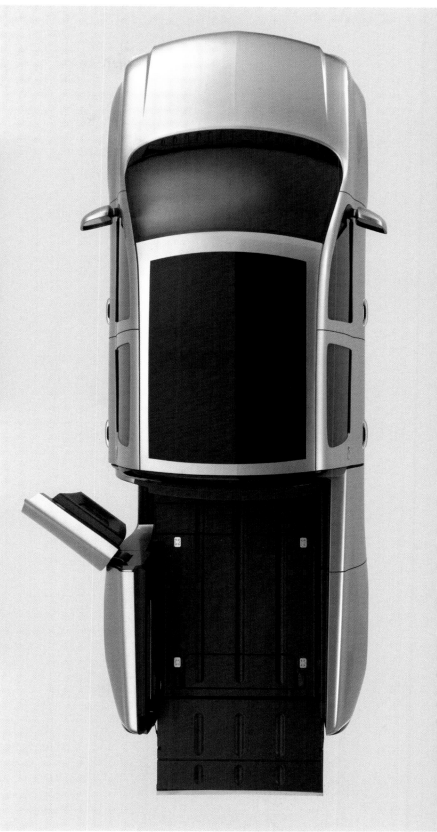

# Chevrolet Colorado

JOEL PLASKOWSKI

| | |
|---|---|
| Design | Clay Dean |
| Engine | 3.5 in-line 5 (2.8 in-line 4 also offered) |
| Power | 164 kW (220 bhp) @ 5600 rpm |
| Torque | 305 Nm (225 lb. ft) @ 2800 rpm |
| Gearbox | 5-speed manual |
| Installation | Front-engined/rear-wheel drive |
| Front suspension | Independent with torsion bar |
| Rear suspension | Live axle with leaf springs |
| Brakes front/rear | Discs/drums |
| Front tires | 205/75R15 |
| Rear tires | 205/75R15 |
| Length | 4887 mm (192.4 in.) |
| Width | 1720 mm (67.7 in.) |
| Height | 1648 mm (64.9 in.) |
| Wheelbase | 2827 mm (111.3 in.) |
| Curb weight | 1541 kg (3397 lb.) |

Chevrolet has an aggressive program launching new trucks, and the new Colorado marks the fifth all-new Chevy truck since the announcement of the Avalanche at the 1999 North American International Auto Show.

At the front, the mix of lights, grilles, air intakes, and body-colored strips gives the Colorado an easily identifiable look, albeit one that is rather cluttered and resoundingly American rather than contemporary and global. An unapologetic gold Chevy "bowtie" badge adorns the grille bar, reflecting the company's truck heritage. And chunky wheel arches with lots of wheel clearance clearly categorize this model as one that will be most at home off-road.

It must be a tough task convincing America's buying public that the GM stable has an excellent new engine that doesn't come in V8 form. The new "I6" and "I5" in-line five-cylinder units launched in the Chevrolet Trailblazer have made significant progress down this path, and it is derivatives of these engines that are used in the new Colorado. The earlier engines have passed on their particularly good power and torque curves—qualities that are ideal for this type of vehicle.

The Colorado comes in three body styles, all based on the same platform. In addition to the crew cab, the body style that accounts for one in three of all midsized pickups sold in the USA, there are the extended cab and the regular cab. The Colorado goes on sale during the last quarter of 2003 as an utterly traditional midsized pickup.

# Chevrolet Equinox

| | |
|---|---|
| Design | Ken Parkinson, Rich Scheer, and Christos Roustemis |
| Engine | 3.4 V6 |
| Power | 138 kW (185 bhp) @ 5200 rpm |
| Torque | 285 Nm (210 lb. ft) @ 3800 rpm |
| Gearbox | 5-speed automatic |
| Installation | Front-engined/all-wheel drive |
| Front suspension | MacPherson strut |
| Rear suspension | Trailing arm |
| Brakes front/rear | Discs/drums |
| Front tires | P235/65R16 |
| Rear tires | P235/65R16 |
| Length | 4757 mm (187.3 in.) |
| Width | 1834 mm (72.2 in.) |
| Height | 1681 mm (66.2 in.) |
| Wheelbase | 2857 mm (112.5 in.) |
| Curb weight | 1634 kg (3602 lb.) |

The new Equinox won't be seen until 2004, but the production version was unveiled early, at the Detroit show in January 2003. It comes complete with both the new Chevrolet look and unmistakable truck DNA.

The all-new Equinox has an altogether softer design than its slightly larger brother, the Colorado pickup, but the proportion is still classic SUV, with chunky features to match. A wide grille, big headlights, and large pillars all make it look strong—and undoubtedly it is. The forward-angled C- and D-pillars give it a dynamic poise which, with a 3.4-liter V6 engine under the hood, it can rightly claim.

When launched, the Equinox will be the largest vehicle in its class, with a wheelbase of 2857 mm (112.5 in.). This gives it the advantage of better passenger comfort and cargo capability. One of the most useful features is Multi-Flex seating, where the rear seat slides by up to 20 cm (8 in.), providing extra room for passengers when moved back, or additional luggage capacity when moved forward. The combination of a fold-flat front passenger seat with a split-folding rear seat also allows extra-long objects to be carried inside. Another useful feature is a height-adjustable cargo shelf that doubles as a security cover and a picnic table.

The Equinox will, no question, help Chevrolet put a strong new competitor into the fastest-growing segment of the market, compact utilities. This segment has breached the one-million sales point for the first time, and this is where the company needs to be.

# Chevrolet Malibu

| | |
|---|---|
| Design | Crystal Wyndham and Sung Paik |
| Engine | 3.5 V6 |
| Power | 149 kW (200 bhp) @ 5400 rpm |
| Torque | 285 Nm (210 lb. ft) @ 3600 rpm |
| Gearbox | 4-speed automatic |
| Installation | Front-engined/front-wheel drive |
| Front suspension | Strut type with stabilizer bar |
| Rear suspension | Independent 4-link with stabilizer bar |
| Brakes front/rear | Discs/drums |
| Front tires | P215/60R16 |
| Rear tires | P215/60R16 |
| Length | 4783 mm (188.3 in.) |
| Width | 1775 mm (69.9 in.) |
| Height | 1461 mm (57.5 in.) |
| Wheelbase | 2700 mm (106.3 in.) |
| Curb weight | 1504 kg (4820 lb.) |

The Malibu is an important new model because it's the first US car based on General Motors' new Epsilon platform. In addition, it is Chevrolet's new midsized sedan aimed at the mass market, and recalls a model name first introduced on a sportier iteration of the Chevelle, a 1960s bestseller for Chevrolet that occupied a similar market slot.

Its design is very unthreatening and conservative, to the point of being almost featureless. Large, taut surfaces end with squared-off corners and are intersected by simple shut-lines to make the overall form look boxy yet, with the chrome front bar complete with gold "bowtie" badge, still distinctively Chevrolet.

Chevrolet promises that the Malibu will, due to its new platform, have excellent ride and handling. This unit is already used as the platform for the new Opel Vectra and Saab 9-3 models in Europe. The platform's design allows the ride to be softened slightly to suit America's more unpredictable road surfaces, so the chances are that the Malibu's road manners won't be as sharp as those of its European siblings.

There is an attempt to tailor the Malibu to the masses by offering greater comfort. This feature memorizes the seat height, the steering wheel tilt/telescopic adjustment, and the positions of the brake and accelerator pedals so that the driver's seating position can be programmed.

A first for this segment of the market is the remote-start package, which allows the driver to start the car from inside the home. This could be a particularly useful feature on winter mornings or sweltering summer afternoons, and the system works over a distance of 60 meters (200 ft).

Motorists who want to blend into the background should note that production of the Malibu is targeted for the third quarter of 2003. This is car design at its most underwhelming.

# Chevrolet SS

| Design | Franz von Holzhausen |
|---|---|
| Engine | 6.0 V8 |
| Power | 320 kW (430 bhp) |
| Torque | 584 Nm (430 lb. ft) |
| Gearbox | 4-speed automatic |
| Installation | Front-engined/rear-wheel drive |
| Front suspension | Short and long arm |
| Rear suspension | Short and long arm |
| Brakes front/rear | Discs/discs |
| Front tires | 255/45R21 |
| Rear tires | 275/45R22 |
| Length | 5052 mm (198.9 in.) |
| Width | 1930 mm (76 in.) |
| Height | 1346 mm (53 in.) |
| Wheelbase | 3150 mm (124 in.) |
| Track front/rear | 1670/1651 mm (65.7/65 in.) |
| Curb weight | 1660 kg (3650 lb.) |

The Chevrolet SS is one of those exotic and emotional concepts that most people drool over while going weak at the knees. Its four-door architecture has a rearward-biased cab design and is shrouded by clean-looking, curvaceous bodywork. It's long, low, and decidedly phallic.

With such a sports car, the wheels are very much the focus of attention. Sweeping wheel arches draw the hungry eye in, closely hugging the tires and therefore signifying the limited suspension on offer, and the hard, sporty ride that will surely result. At the back, circular taillights project sportiness but in a modern way, with no fuss.

The SS, designed in GM's Los Angeles studio, is painted in victory red and fitted with reflective Cromax glass. The interior is similarly clean-looking, with hints of the heritage of the fabled Camaro SS, one of the first "muscle cars" of the late 1960s. Stark off-white and slate leather surfaces contrast with the warm, red exterior. The seat upholstery is also a blast from the past: a mixture of white leather and a modern woven, houndstooth-check vinyl.

A welcome technology for saving fuel is the SS's "Displacement on Demand" system, which makes its debut in 2004 on some production models. This shuts down half of the cylinders during most driving conditions and automatically reactivates them for demanding use such as brisk acceleration or towing.

Chevrolet has a great sporting heritage with its iconic Corvette and Camaro. The SS, however, somehow looks more sophisticated than many of its past offerings. This is the closest thing yet to an American version of Ferrari's 456.

# Chrysler Airflite

| Design | Greg Howell and Simeon Kim |
|---|---|
| Engine | 3.5 V6 |
| Installation | Front-engined/rear-wheel drive |
| Front tires | 235/45R20 |
| Rear tires | 255/45R21 |
| Length | 4838 mm (190.4 in.) |
| Width | 1870 mm (73.6 in.) |
| Height | 1448 mm (57 in.) |
| Wheelbase | 2946 mm (116 in.) |
| Track front/rear | 1600/1630 mm (63/64.2 in.) |

Now that other Chrysler models, such as the Pacifica and the Crossfire, are in the hands of appreciative customers, the company's new design language is developing one stage further with the new Airflite concept. This sporty five-door coupé represents a fresh interpretation of Chrysler's automotive face, with its bold grille and distinctive headlights giving a strong impression of precision engineering.

The A-pillars rise sharply from a hood that boasts lively feature lines, three either side of the distinctive spine that runs the length of the car. From the top of the windshield the roofline tapers down to the boat-tail at the back of the car, largely repeating the Crossfire's form. The tail is finished with a bold wing badge made of chrome.

In creating the Airflite, the designers took inspiration from contemporary furniture, classic boats, and the Art Deco Chrysler Building in New York. Continuous radii and ovals are noticeably used in conjunction with straight lines for features and surfaces.

Nautical themes inspire the interior, but the overall look is chiseled and architectural—that is, functional but not particularly comfortable. A brushed-metal center spine dominates, connecting the interior from front to back, but it contrasts sharply with the natural look of the wooden floor, which is accented with brushed-aluminum strips to protect the wood and to echo the center console. The satin silver-colored center console seems to form a structural member tying together the two sides of the car.

All a touch radical for now, perhaps, but Chrysler's concept cars have a pleasing habit of hitting the road if it's thought customers are willing to buy them.

# Chrysler California Cruiser

| Design | Trevor Creed |
|---|---|
| Engine | 2.4 in-line 4 |
| Gearbox | Autostick |
| Installation | Front-engined/rear-wheel drive |
| Brakes front/rear | Discs/discs |
| Front tires | 225/35R19 |
| Rear tires | 225/35R19 |
| Length | 4290 mm (168.9 in.) |
| Width | 1725 mm (67.9 in.) |
| Height | 1511 mm (59.5 in.) |
| Wheelbase | 2616 mm (103 in.) |
| Track front/rear | 1481/1478 mm (58.3/58.2 in.) |
| Curb weight | 1454 kg (3206 lb.) |

You could be forgiven for thinking this is simply a PT Cruiser "refresh," but in fact the California Cruiser is an all-new concept. It draws heavily, of course, on the design of the PT Cruiser, which has been on sale now for three years, but it has a much more modern feel compared with its stablemate's deeply retro design.

The proportions are pretty similar to the PT's, but the California Cruiser is harder-edged, sporting contemporary silver body-side and tailgate panels. The rear is wrapped by several horizontal silver lines that give a crisp look and echo the prominent slats on the grille. One key feature of the concept, quite apart from its large load-carrying capacity, is the retractable top. This has eight glass panels that lower or pivot to create fresh-air fun, as well as drop-down door glass and swiveling quarter-lights—a detail much loved by drivers with memories of 1950s cars—to let that LA sunshine flood in.

The California Cruiser shows a new face to Chrysler design, with scalloped headlights, a chrome-accentuated grille, and an integrated bumper that reflects the detail design of both the new Crossfire and the soon-to-emerge Pacifica.

Inside, keynote horizontal elements are continued in the form of silver inserts on the door trim, quarter panels, and hatchback lining, and this emphasizes the interior volume. For an ostensibly old-fashioned-looking car, the California Cruiser turns out to be pleasingly contemporary.

The modular seats have retractable head restraints, making the seats compact enough to be folded totally flat. Chrysler, however, never misses a trick for eye-catching trinkets: the winged Chrysler badge, in chrome, is set into the back of each seat.

The success of the PT Cruiser has been so important to an often-embattled Chrysler that the company is anxious to capitalize on any similar ideas; the California Cruiser proves it still has plenty of inspiration to mine.

# Chrysler Pacifica

| | |
|---|---|
| Design | Trevor Creed |
| Engine | 3.5 V6 |
| Gearbox | 4-speed automatic |
| Installation | Front-engined/all-wheel drive |
| Front suspension | MacPherson strut |
| Rear suspension | Multi-link |
| Brakes front/rear | Discs/discs, TCS |
| Front tires | 235/65R17 |
| Rear tires | 235/65R17 |
| Length | 5052 mm (198.9 in.) |
| Width | 2014 mm (79.3 in.) |
| Height | 1689 mm (66.5 in.) |
| Wheelbase | 2954 mm (116.3 in.) |
| Track front/rear | 1676/1676 mm (66/66 in.) |

In keeping with its growing tradition, Chrysler has taken another exciting concept vehicle and put it into production. Launched in buyer-ready form at the New York International Auto Show in 2002, the Pacifica represents a new vehicle segment called "sports tourer." Thanks to the design leadership of Trevor Creed, Chrysler now has an exciting range of cars in its showrooms and has tripled its market share over the past ten years. The Pacifica is the latest model in a recent line of innovative new products that includes the Prowler, PT Cruiser, and Crossfire, and looks set to emulate their groundbreaking progress.

The production version of the Pacifica remains largely true to the original concept featured in *The Car Design Yearbook 1*, with only a few minor changes made to the headlight detail, door moldings, and handles. The lower body is now black, giving a marginally more rugged look despite the fact that the wheels are smaller. Chrysler believes there is nothing quite like the Pacifica in the marketplace, and, while the BMW X5 offers strong competition, the Pacifica, with its low step-in height and three rows of seats, is a far more practical proposition for many Americans.

And this is a top-end car, too. Luxury seating, a navigation system, hands-free communication, and a power tailgate are all features to ensure the Pacifica can snatch sales from the best of the SUVs.

# Citroën C-Airdream

| Engine | 3.0 V6 |
|---|---|
| Power | 157 kW (210 bhp) @ 6100 rpm |
| Gearbox | Auto-adaptive automatic |
| Installation | Front-engined/front-wheel drive |
| Front suspension | Hydractive |
| Rear suspension | Hydractive |
| Length | 4499 mm (177.1 in.) |
| Width | 1915 mm (75.4 in.) |
| Height | 1289 mm (50.7 in.) |
| Wheelbase | 2725 mm (107.3 in.) |
| Track front/rear | 1747/1727 mm (68.8/68 in.) |

Citroën's gorgeous C-Airdream concept is a beautifully crafted masterpiece. This design for a new sports coupé has a sleek, aerodynamic shape, with a rearward-biased proportion, and detailing that exudes sportiness and promises real enjoyment. You can't help thinking the spirit of the idiosyncratic but stunning 1970 Citroën SM has been crafted into a loving homage.

The car's "face" is dominated by two large, slotted air intakes and narrow, swept-back headlights that sit either side of the famous double-chevron grille. The sculpted hood rises gently to the steeply raked windshield and this line continues up to the panoramic glass roof, giving occupants a feeling of complete openness. The roof panel gradually falls to the rear, ending abruptly as the body waists inward to reduce aerodynamic drag—an SM touch for certain.

A subtle mix of dark, glossy, and matt leather flows throughout the cabin, so that the interior oozes a sculptural surface language reminiscent of a sultry cocktail bar. The moiré-look seats are refreshingly different and look amply comfortable.

As with Citroën's previous concept car, the C-Crosser, there is a technology focus on drive-by-wire systems. On the C-Airdream, controls for accelerator, brakes, and gear change are all located on the steering wheel, completely eliminating the need for a pedal box. This in turn gives more scope for interior design and improves safety. Even the steering actuation is via electronic control systems, obviating the need for conventional mechanical parts.

If only Citroën had the nerve to produce this car—as it did the SM— it would surely connect with a very chic audience, and bring to market a car that is in many ways truly new and exciting.

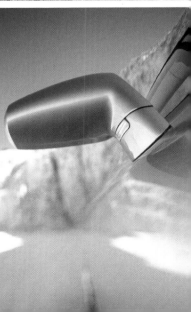

# Daewoo Flex

The Flex is a large MPV that is as big as the new Renault Espace and features similarly large wheels and low ground clearance. Its exterior design is executed more successfully than Daewoo's recently released Oto concept, with clean lines, and a better grille and front light design.

The dark-gray graphical theme at the front is copied from the 2001 Kalos and 1998 Mirae concepts but needs further resolution. The short hood and cab-forward profile, however, allow the occupants to sit up front, while the A-pillars quickly rise to give an elegant flowing arc up on to the roof. Concentric feature lines around front and rear wheels run horizontally, fading out before the door handles. They contribute to the car's most distinctive feature: its side view.

At the rear are more references to Renault design proportions: the lower trunk sits rearward of the rear windshield, which, in turn, wraps around to the body sides.

Inside, the Flex is impractical, with metallic seats offering no lateral support—the sort of thing more normally found in airport terminals than luxurious cars. Also, the instrument panel is far too austere and needs to be rethought for typical MPV customers.

With some redesign, particularly inside, the Flex could be a successful Daewoo entry into the crowded MPV sector; GM's new backing gives plenty of donor platforms to choose from. But present-day rivals are totally focussed on practicality, not trashy design details. Daewoo also desperately needs a clear product identity to reflect its corporate image. There is still much work to do here.

| Design | GM Daewoo Auto & Technology Co. in Korea |
|---|---|
| Engine | V6 diesel |
| Power | 191kW (256 bhp) @ 3600 rpm |
| Torque | 408 Nm (301 lb. ft) @ 2000 rpm |
| Length | 4673 mm (184 in.) |
| Width | 1997 mm (78.6 in.) |
| Height | 1720 mm (67.7 in.) |
| Wheelbase | 2870 mm (113 in.) |

# Daewoo Nubira

| | |
|---|---|
| Design | Pininfarina |
| Engine | 1.6 in-line 4 (1.8 in-line 4 also offered) |
| Power | 122 kW (164 bhp) @ 5800 rpm |
| Torque | 165 Nm (122 lb. ft) @ 4000 rpm |
| Gearbox | 5-speed manual |
| Installation | Front engined/front-wheel drive |
| Front suspension | MacPherson strut |
| Rear suspension | Dual link |
| Brakes front/rear | Discs/discs |
| Front tires | 195/55R15 |
| Rear tires | 195/55R15 |
| Length | 4500 mm (177.2 in.) |
| Width | 1725 mm (67.9 in.) |
| Height | 1445 mm (56.9 in.) |
| Wheelbase | 2600 mm (102.4 in.) |
| Track front/rear | 1480/1480 mm (58.3/58.3 in.) |
| Curb weight | 1210 kg (2668 lb.) |
| 0–100 km/h (62 mph) | 9.5 sec |
| Top speed | 195 km/h (121 mph) |
| Fuel consumption | 7.5 ltr/100 km (31.4 mpg) |
| $CO_2$ emissions | 183 g/km |

The new Nubira, named the Lacetti in South Korea, was designed by Pininfarina in Italy, and immediately gives the impression of a much sharper effort than the resolutely mediocre outgoing model. This is the second Daewoo to emerge since General Motors took control of the brand and most of its assets; first was the Kalos, which was reviewed very favorably in the press. When complete, the Nubira range will consist of a sedan, a fastback, and an estate model.

Still, the new Nubira is conservatively designed and conceived to be offered at a competitive price. It is slightly larger than a European lower-medium-sized car, and prices will be pitched just above a typical European small car like the Volkswagen Golf.

More modern than in the previous model, the interior uses higher-quality moldings and materials, and the development team is confident of achieving a four-star NCAP safety rating. This will all help to boost the perception of Daewoo as a first-world, rather than a third-world, brand.

The old Nubira suffered terrible deterioration in ride quality. If the new, sharper lines and Eurocentric styling turn out to be coupled with better dynamics from more thorough engineering standards, then Daewoo could challenge the market share of the likes of Skoda and Ford.

GM's protracted move to control Daewoo was a smart idea. Daewoo's low-cost South Korean base and range of vehicle platforms will suit the American giant's products in developing countries. GM will make a success of Daewoo if it can squeeze every last ounce of value from its low-cost platforms while also improving the brand strength, just as VW did with Skoda throughout the 1990s.

# Daewoo Scope

| | |
|---|---|
| **Design** | GM Daewoo Auto & Technology Co. in Korea |
| **Engine** | 2.5 in-line 6 |
| **Power** | 157 kW (211 bhp) @ 5800 rpm |
| **Torque** | 245 Nm (181 lb. ft) @ 4000 rpm |
| **Length** | 4474 mm (176.1 in.) |
| **Width** | 1897 mm (74.7 in.) |
| **Height** | 1710 mm (67.3 in.) |
| **Wheelbase** | 2650 mm (104.3 in.) |

Originally launched as the Oto at the Seoul Motor Show in 2002, the Scope is the most recent name to adorn Daewoo's new SUV concept. This fresh vision for a lifestyle vehicle shares some of its angular features with the Flex concept and would compete in the very design-led SUV marketplace, where Chrysler and BMW are well established. Does Daewoo have the brand strength to compete here? Probably not, but the Scope offers classic SUV proportions with high ground clearance. Features designed to make the car look sporty yet tough include the arched rear window, the rising wedge along the length of the doors, the chunky wheels, and the large wheel clearances enhanced by cunningly applied black trim.

The rectangular grille, with vertical veins, provides a new look for the make; still, it is a pity a strong corporate face—one that is consistent across its range—has not yet emerged from Daewoo.

The Scope's seven-seater interior is designed to be flexible, with versatile seating that can be moved around to optimize space. New technology is featured too: remote-control functions include starting the engine, opening and closing doors, and operating audiovisual systems via a pop-up wide screen. Navigation with live traffic information is relayed directly to the instrument panel.

Further resolution is needed to make this design a winning hybrid, combining all-terrain ability and the excitement of a sports coupé. The SUV sector is set to grow, but we must wait to see if Daewoo will take a gamble with the Scope in this luxury- and design-conscious market where the BMW X5 is the yardstick of desirability.

# Dodge Avenger

| | |
|---|---|
| Design | Trevor Creed |
| Engine | 3.5 V6 |
| Gearbox | 4-speed automatic |
| Installation | Front-engined/all-wheel drive |
| Front tires | 265/55R20 |
| Rear tires | 295/50R20 |
| Length | 4754 mm (187.2 in.) |
| Width | 1836 mm (72.3 in.) |
| Height | 1616 mm (63.6 in.) |
| Wheelbase | 2870 mm (113 in.) |
| Track front/rear | 1554/1554 mm (61.2/61.2 in.) |

The objective of the Dodge Avenger project was to merge European-style "rally-car" performance and style with some of the convenience and capability of the American SUV. European rally cars such as the Subaru Impreza and Peugeot 206 appear to be highly rated in the USA for their performance and toughness but are usually only ever seen here in video games.

Dodge took some key rally-car elements for the design of the Avenger: robust, angular wings and lower door trim; high ground clearance with body-colored sills; and an overall chiseled look. Part of the Dodge brand philosophy is that it should offer the consumer more than the competition, and the Avenger concept attempts this mainly by including four doors, the rear ones opening out to ninety degrees for good access, a large tailgate, and, of course, all-wheel drive and all-road capability. These last two essentials already sit comfortably with Dodge's American SUV customers.

The Avenger's interior is sparse, with vinyl flooring and black and silver accents betraying a driver-focused environment. There are body-hugging seats, too, all with four-point harnesses.

With the Avenger, Dodge is aiming at a young and aspirational market while simultaneously trying to rekindle some excitement in what is otherwise a dowdy brand image. European rally teams should be flattered to have provided the inspiration—if they notice this contrived hybrid.

# Dodge Durango

| | |
|---|---|
| Design | Trevor Creed |
| Engine | 5.7 V8 |
| Power | 257 kW (345 bhp) @ 5400 rpm |
| Torque | 509 Nm (375 lb. ft) @ 4200 rpm |
| Gearbox | 5-speed automatic |
| Installation | Front-engined/four-wheel drive |
| Front suspension | Multi-link |
| Rear suspension | Solid axle, coil springs |
| Front tires | 265/50R21 |
| Rear tires | 265/50R21 |
| Length | 5009 mm (197.2 in.) |
| Width | 1943 mm (76.5 in.) |
| Height | 1824 mm (71.8 in.) |
| Wheelbase | 3028 mm (119.2 in.) |
| Track front/rear | 1636/1636 mm (64.4/64.4 in.) |

The Dodge Durango concept provides a strong hint of the next-generation Durango, which will appear in late 2003. Dodge says it represents 85% of the finished production-level exterior design. The current Durango is already a huge truck, but this new concept is at least 7.5 cm (3 in.) taller still, as well as being wider. It has more interior space and can carry seven people. The enlarged cargo deck can now hold standard-sized plasterboard, which is 122 cm (48 in.) wide—good news for America's builders.

Presence and power are easy to portray when you have a 5.7-liter engine and a truck of just over 5 meters (16.4 ft) long. Even so, the massive cross-hair grille and snorting air intakes on the hood make this one of the most masculine-looking trucks on the market.

Dodge, however, has been diligent in ensuring the Durango is also sporty, and not too agricultural. Short overhangs, aluminum sill guards and roof rails, and a raked windshield all contribute, as does a gently rising waistline. The lower body highlights its off-road capability: protective guards front and rear, and distinctive, bulging wheel arches with plenty of tire clearance for off-road suspension articulation.

The interior follows some clear geometric rules. Surfaces are constructed using constant radii for a simple overall form and, perhaps, a little rural ruggedness. But dark slate leather and an absence of wooden trim give the cabin a rather cold look.

# Dodge Kahuna

| Design | Trevor Creed |
|---|---|
| Engine | 2.4 in-line 4 turbocharged |
| Power | 160 kW (215 bhp) |
| Gearbox | 4-speed automatic |
| Installation | Front-engined/front-wheel drive |
| Front suspension | MacPherson strut |
| Rear suspension | Coil springs |
| Front tires | 255/5OR22 |
| Rear tires | 255/5OR22 |
| Length | 4714 mm (185.6 in.) |
| Width | 1976 mm (77.8 in.) |
| Height | 1702 mm (67 in.) |
| Wheelbase | 3099 mm (122 in.) |
| Track front/rear | 1659/1659 mm (65.3/65.3 in.) |

The Kahuna concept is specifically designed for California's coastal culture. After all, Californians buy a lot of cars and are a fashion-conscious bunch. The Kahuna has enough space to seat six but can easily be adapted to carry more beach gear and fewer people.

There are some obvious design similarities to the Chrysler California Cruiser (see p. 64), but the Dodge is essentially a cool-looking people-carrier, something that is often difficult to achieve because of the limitations of the necessarily boxy shape. Rather than a sliding rear door it has a conventionally hinged one, but with the upper frames and structure removed. This means the Kahuna can be driven totally open at the side when all the windows are dropped.

The Kahuna is a mono-volume design, to maximize interior space. The exterior is finished in Point Break blue, with accents of composite bird's-eye-maple laminate along the side panels. The sliding roof is made from a silver-gray canvas that is both water-resistant and transparent.

The front end features a pared-down interpretation of Dodge's cross-hair grille. Although just about recognizable, this design just doesn't have the beauty and finesse of the car's side profile, with its delicate horizontal lines. The chunky wheel arches look great, however, and project a youthful, go-anywhere spirit. Inside, the "big wave" theme continues throughout, in two tones of blue. A wave design is used to shape the instrument panel as well as the switches, door-panel detailing and seats.

It would be fantastic to see fun design like this make it to car showrooms across the USA, but it's highly unlikely a business case could ever be made for such a limited-market car. A darned shame.

# Dodge Magnum SRT-8

| | |
|---|---|
| Design | Trevor Creed |
| Engine | 5.7 V8 |
| Power | 320 kW (430 bhp) @ 5600 rpm |
| Torque | 651 Nm (480 lb. ft) @ 4000 rpm |
| Gearbox | 5-speed automatic |
| Front suspension | Short and long arm |
| Rear suspension | Multi-link |
| Front tires | 275/40R20 |
| Rear tires | 295/40R20 |
| Length | 5021 mm (197.7 in.) |
| Width | 1880 mm (74 in.) |
| Height | 1505 mm (59.3 in.) |
| Wheelbase | 3048 mm (120 in.) |
| Track front/rear | 1600/1600 mm (63/63 in.) |
| Curb weight | 1808 kg (3986 lb.) |

The Magnum SRT-8 Concept is a fitting addition to the design vocabulary of the company that gave us the iconic Ram truck and Viper sports car. This new sports tourer clearly reflects Dodge's American "muscle" design background and comes complete with a Hemi engine.

Its on-the-road presence and projection of power are highlighted by the Dodge "face," with its huge grille, and the low bodywork, which makes the doors, in particular, appear deep and strong. Overall, there is a chiseled form to the body, with large surfaces broken by two-dimensional lines. The result is a purposeful look created by changes in light reflection.

The wheels are a very strong feature: deeply dished, chunky five-spokes lurking under distinctive wheel arches that embrace them. A wide-opening tailgate that hinges forward of the rear pillar offers proper cargo flexibility.

The seating position is 6 cm (2.4 in.) higher than in the conventional Dodge car range because people are now accustomed to SUV-style seating. Four competition-style instrument gauges with machined aluminum trim rings are tunneled in, like the Dodge Viper's. The Magnum SRT-8 also features Viper-inspired racing-style pedals of drilled aluminum.

Interior leather is dark slate gray with ochre accents. Three brushed-aluminum spokes radiate from an aluminum ram's head in the center of the steering wheel, with the vertical spoke replicating the split spokes of the exterior wheels.

With a vast array of platforms at Dodge's disposal, and such a well-refined design as this to attach to one of them, it's likely this model will see production.

# Ferrari Enzo

| Design | Pininfarina |
|---|---|
| Engine | 6.0 V12 |
| Power | 485 kW (660 bhp) @ 7800 rpm |
| Torque | 657 Nm (484 lb. ft) @ 5500 rpm |
| Installation | Mid-engined |
| Brakes front/rear | Discs/discs |
| Front tires | 245/40ZR19 |
| Rear tires | 345/35ZR19 |
| Length | 4720 mm (185.8 in.) |
| Width | 2035 mm (80.1 in.) |
| Height | 1147 mm (45.2 in.) |
| Wheelbase | 2650 mm (104.3 in.) |
| Track front/rear | 1660 mm/1650 (65.4/65 in.) |
| Curb weight | 1365 kg (3009 lb.) |
| 0–100 km/h (62 mph) | 3.65 sec |
| Top speed | 350 km/h (218mph) |

Named after Ferrari's legendary founder (although industry rumors initially suggested that it was to be called the F60), the new Enzo is the latest V12 supercar from the Italian maker. Ferrari and Michael Schumacher have so dominated Formula One over the past four years that in 2002 their success led to a reassessment of the rules with the aim of making the sport more competitive. So there can hardly have been a better time for a dominant Ferrari to launch a new F1-inspired road car.

Pininfarina is the design consultancy responsible for every production Ferrari over the past four decades, with the exception of the 1973–80 Bertone-designed Dino 308GT4. Naturally, this great studio was commissioned to style this latest model.

As with all supercars of this nature, aerodynamics are intrinsic to the car's function and style; indeed, the Enzo is an extreme example of this emphasis. Its body is made from carbon fiber and Nomex composite, allowing Pininfarina's designers the freedom to create optimized surfaces that would be absolutely impossible with conventional metal pressings.

At the front, the Enzo sports an F1-style raised nose and two massive intakes that channel air up to the brakes and over the windshield. The cockpit is small, to minimize drag, and tapers at the rear on to a flat section before finishing abruptly at the rear edge. The absence of a conventional rear airfoil is possible because of the huge venturis sitting between the rear wheels. These speed up the escaping air and pull the car down hard to the road surface.

Inside, it is a tight squeeze, with acres of visible carbon fiber that concentrates the mind on functional dedication rather than mere comfort.

This is an extreme Ferrari, dedicated to performance, and it does not have the beautiful aesthetics of models like the 360 Modena. A limited production run of 399 Enzos is planned, but if you want one it's already too late: they have all been sold.

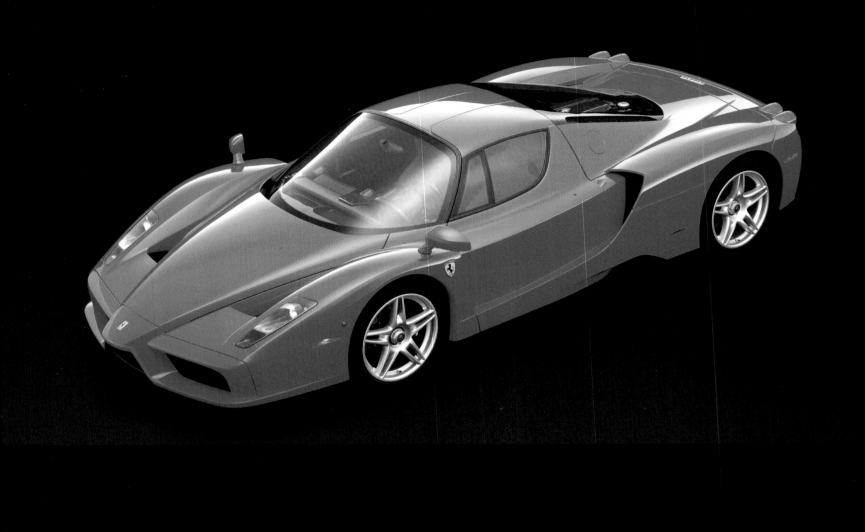

# Fiat Gingo

The Fiat Gingo is a well-resolved compact car that replaces Fiat's current small cars, the anodyne Seicento and the positively antediluvian Panda. However, unlike the two models it supplants, it comes in only a five-door version. And, in contrast to those two, it can seat five, at a squeeze.

This is a simple yet audacious design in the Fiat tradition that began with the original Topolino back in 1936. It makes playful use of chrome grilles, arches, and conventional rectangular shapes. The front, though, is pretty conservative, almost Volkswagen-like in its normality, while below the waistline the side profile matches the tops of the doors. These arch to the rear, where there's a square quarter-light that, thanks to clever design, makes the Gingo appear much bigger from the side than it actually is. The back end resembles nothing so much as a smaller Fiat Multipla, with a big, rectangular rear windshield that curves and wraps up at the top. The huge rear lights are extremely practical and should give the Gingo a strong presence at night.

Inside are several features new to small Fiats. In another reinterpretation of the Multipla, the gearshift now pokes out of the center of the dashboard to improve ergonomics for the driver. There's a big, transparent Skydome roof, the choice of manual or automatic climate control, a parking sensor at the rear, and a folding rear seat.

The Gingo was launched in Europe in March 2003, at the Geneva International Motor Show, and needs to be a major success for the embattled company. One problem may be the fact that small, cheap cars typically make little profit for manufacturers, but Fiat is hoping the Gingo's high-level interior specifications, cunning use of so-called "upmarket" chrome trimmings, and a shape that suggests a lot of (small) car for the money will justify the slight premium it is charging for this all-European rival to the likes of the Daewoo Matiz and Toyota Yaris.

| | |
|---|---|
| Design | Fiat Centro Stile and Bertone |
| Engine | 1.3 in-line 4 (1.1 and 1.2 in-line 4 also offered) |
| Power | 52 kW (70 bhp) |
| Gearbox | 5-speed manual |
| Installation | Front-engined/front-wheel drive |
| Brakes front/rear | Discs/discs, ABS, EBD |
| Length | 3540 mm (139.4 in.) |
| Width | 1580 mm (62.2 in.) |
| Height | 1530 mm (60.2 in.) |

# Fiat Idea

| Design | Fiat Centro Stile and Italdesign |
|---|---|
| Engine | 1.4 in-line 4 (1.2 and 1.3 in-line 4, and 1.9 in-line 4 diesel, also offered) |
| Installation | Front-engined/front-wheel drive |
| Brakes front/rear | Discs/discs, ABS, EBD, BA |
| Length | 4000 mm (157.5 in.) |
| Width | 1700 mm (66.9 in.) |
| Height | 1660 mm (65.4 in.) |
| Wheelbase | 2510 mm (98.8 in.) |

The Fiat Idea is much less whimsical in its conception than the smaller Gingo. Based on the mainstream Punto, it is a more serious mini-MPV that simply adopts the Punto's cab-forward proportions. This design called for a forward quarter-light in front of the front door, as in the Renault Espace, to facilitate the car's key selling point: a higher roofline to maximize interior space.

The front of the Idea is similar to that of the Stilo. Large headlights, a body-colored bumper, and a dark grille are an attractive combination. Big doors and a cut-back sill make the Idea look light and nimble, characteristics that are exaggerated by sporty, slightly flared wheel arches.

Inside, the design is masterly, with centrally aligned instruments and clearly labeled, ergonomically set-up switchgear. The colors are warm and friendly, creating a typically French ambience rather than a flamboyant Italian or somber German one. In this market, interior features that increase comfort are important, and the Idea serves up the goods: it comes with cruise control, an adjustable steering wheel, a sliding rear seat, an elevated driving position, and a high roofline. These aren't especially innovative features, though, so the Idea must rely on its design and low cost to draw in sales. Fiats have been funky and cheap before, but the market has tired of this simple combination in recent years, so let's hope interest can be rekindled.

The Idea is going on sale across Europe between the autumn of 2003 and early 2004. This new market niche of mini-MPV is expected to continue growing, but fierce initial competition will come from the excellent new Opel Meriva.

# Fiat Marrakech

Based on the Fiat Gingo, the open-top Marrakech would be brilliant fun in countries where it doesn't rain much—Morocco, for example, home to the city that inspired the car's name.

It was created by the Idea Institute in Italy, and is designed purely to get people excited about the possibilities for the new Gingo—a well-worn marketing stunt often revived when Fiat launches a major new car. At the debut of the Cinquecento in 1992, for example, a flotilla of eight "fun" concept cars from Italian design consultancies was used to inject a little verve into the proceedings.

Design-wise, the Marrakech's exterior shares the hood, front grille, and lights with the Gingo, but there is a new front bumper, with what appears to be a large plastic protector in the center, to give the car a more adventurous feel. Along the sides there are no doors, just a high sill complete with a grab rail to provide stiffness to the body, to give protection in side impacts and to act as a useful support when climbing into the car.

The lower surfaces around the rear are almost identical to the Gingo's, but the lights have been modified to include circular treatments to the white reflectors. There's also a protective guard in the rear bumper to increase durability. The dashboard is taken straight from the Gingo but features new colors to key in with the bright-green exterior paintwork.

It would be marvelous to see fun cars like this on the streets, but the potential market is much too small for Fiat to consider making one. Still, one of the smaller coachbuilders might find the Marrakech feasible as a low-volume, high-price successor to the long-lamented Mini Moke and Citroën Mehari.

| Design | Idea Institute |
| --- | --- |

# Fiat Simba

| Design | Fiat Centro Stile |
|---|---|
| Engine | 1.3 in-line 4 diesel |
| Installation | Front-engined/4-wheel drive |
| Brakes front/rear | Discs/discs |
| Length | 3680 mm (144.9 in.) |
| Width | 1630 mm (64.2 in.) |
| Height | 1730 mm (68.1 in.) |

A new mini off-roader, the Simba concept made its debut at the Bologna Motor Show in Italy. This is a comparatively minor event, but it had an important role in presenting a design preview of the new small Fiat car that will replace the Seicento and the venerable, twenty-two-year-old Panda in 2004.

With a modern, youthful, and fun image, this bold little machine is clothed in 4×4 regalia and looks well protected for any off-road jaunt. At the front there are an imposing bull bar, integrated fog lights and headlights that sit within a molded shield, and large bumpers. Rising from the base of the windshield are two roof rails that encapsulate two further driving lights, adding to the adventurous feel, even if the effect is to recall the slightly laughable Matra Rancho of the late 1970s. The roof rails form an exo-skeletal structure, making the Simba look a bit top-heavy, especially as the spare wheel is roof-mounted.

The choice of body colors accentuates the protective nature of the car. Bright-yellow, chunky wheel arches and door moldings sit proud of the body, acting as a warning to other motorists.

Powered by a 1.3-liter diesel engine and a 4×4 drivetrain, the Simba reintroduces Fiat to four-wheel drive, building on the tradition of the 1980s Panda 4×4.

The Simba is certainly not a car you would use to navigate the globe, but city traffic, yes. It's more of a superficial miniature of the Camel Trophy Land Rover, just a fun experiment in adapting a city car with an entertaining new angle. You can see exactly why Fiat chose Bologna as a local, low-key testing ground for it.

# Ford 427

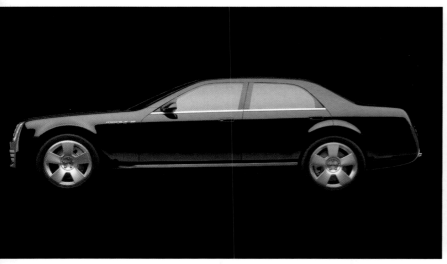

| | |
|---|---|
| Engine | 7.0 V10 |
| Power | 440 kW (590 bhp) @ 6500 rpm |
| Torque | 690 Nm (509 lb. ft) @ 5500 rpm |
| Gearbox | 6-speed manual |
| Front tires | 245/45R19 |
| Rear tires | 245/45R19 |
| Length | 4760 mm (187.4 in.) |
| Width | 1846 mm (72.7 in.) |
| Height | 1344 mm (52.9 in.) |
| Wheelbase | 2872 mm (113 in.) |

Cool American cars such as the Ford Galaxie and LTD enjoyed their heyday in the 1960s. These days hatchbacks and SUVs dominate the scene. Yet, with the 427, Ford has chosen to remind us that it's still possible to create a modern interpretation of the desirable 1960s sedan by using classic proportions: long and low as you can get, with a distinctive three-box shape, and with large, uninterrupted surfaces separated by gentle lines.

Black is excellent for presenting a car that has such a terrifying presence, although the silver trim adds a touch of humanity. The wide grille emphasizes the width of the car and runs outboard to the vertical rectangular headlights. The hood lines are taut and hostile, and everything is magnified by the squareness of the proportions.

Inside, there's no letup to the sinister nature of this car. Black leather with white stitching and brushed aluminum and chrome mix to highly dramatic effect. Gently flowing surfaces and a lack of clutter harmonize well with the exterior design.

The instrument cluster has a TV-screen-shaped speedometer and tachometer with a design that relates directly to that of the front and rear lights. These analog gauges look frustratingly unclear and their red glow is prioritized well ahead of any functionality.

It's bewildering how, in a country where the speed limit is mostly no more than 97 km/h (60 mph), a 7-liter car can be anything but ridiculous, but with retro design so recently fashionable, the 427 definitely got its share of attention at the Detroit show. Which is, of course, its raison d'être.

# Ford F-150

| Design | Craig Metros |
|---|---|
| Engine | 5.4 V8 |
| Power | 224 kW (300 bhp) |
| Installation | Front-engined/all-wheel drive |
| Front tires | P215/60R16 |
| Rear tires | P215/60R16 |

The new F-150 from Ford is the replacement for a model that has led the sales leagues in full-sized pickups for an amazing twenty-six years. The F-150 has long been the USA's bestselling passenger vehicle, and Ford wants the new one to be regarded as not just a tough, utilitarian workhorse but also a comfortable and refined automobile.

The exterior is chunky and powerful, with bold proportions and features. At the front, the large, inverted trapezoidal grille and square headlights dominate, together with a blue 23-cm (9-in.) oval badge, which looks slightly oversized at first but is in fact designed to be in proportion to the huge front end.

Deriving some inspiration from the 2002 F-350 Tonka concept truck, the F-150 uses similarly taut and chiseled shapes. But it features a "waterline": a line extending the length of the vehicle and joining the tops of the front and rear bumpers to create a visual separation around the entire vehicle. This waterline creates visual differentiation between the F-150's five different production ranges—for example, as part of a two-tone paint treatment—while maintaining a design coherence.

The tailgate uses torsion-beam technology, so when it's lowered it feels more like lightweight aluminum or a composite panel than the relentlessly old-tech steel-reinforced tailgate it actually is.

Inside, there are vertical bands, which again allowed the design team to use different colors, textures, and materials for range customization. The theme is quite contemporary and precise, with masses of aluminum and black, while the instrument design and layout faintly recall an aircraft cockpit.

# Ford Faction

| | |
|---|---|
| Design | Kris Tomasson |
| Engine | 2.0 in-line 4 |
| Power | 125 kW (167 bhp) |
| Torque | 194 Nm (143 lb. ft) |
| Installation | Front-engined/all-wheel drive |
| Brakes front/rear | Discs/discs |
| Length | 3900 mm (153.5 in.) |
| Width | 1750 mm (68.9 in.) |
| Height | 1540 mm (60.6 in.) |
| Track front/rear | 1480/1504 mm (58.3/59.2 in.) |
| Curb weight | 1300 kg (2866 lb.) |

Ford's glittering new London-based design studio, engagingly called Ingeni, has been set up with the backing of J. Mays, Ford's Vice President of Design, to study design and cultural trends in this cosmopolitan European city. The Faction is the first new concept car to emerge from the studio.

Unsurprisingly, it sets out to be a lifestyle car for people living in the heart of a crowded urban landscape. Key aims were that it should be functional, nimble, and fashionable. The SUV exterior combines Ford's crisp design language with a dash of ruggedness, to give the car appropriate "attitude."

The design of the Faction concept is based on the idea of making life with a car in the city easier. As London is the first major city to introduce congestion charging, this is timely. A city-friendly door system uses double-link hinges to make getting in and out of the car much easier. Pressing a button on the keyfob, even from a distance, causes the circular door handle to present itself to the driver, indicating that the doors have been unlocked.

The tailgate has a low opening line and incorporates retractable glass that is activated by the keyfob. This feature allows smaller items to be loaded into the back of the vehicle without needing to open the tailgate. The interior was inspired by contemporary furniture. Ingeni's designers were strongly influenced by trends at Europe's annual Milan Furniture Fair, and as a result the Faction concept features clean, simple shapes and muted colors.

To make urban parking a whole lot easier, multiple cameras take images from strategically placed interior and exterior locations. The images are displayed on three screens at the base of the windshield. The driver can choose between a panoramic rear view, a close-up view directly behind the vehicle that includes a security sweep, or a glimpse of the entertaining antics of his passengers.

# Ford Focus C-Max

| Design | Chris Bird |
|---|---|
| Engine | 2.0 in-line 4 diesel (1.6 in-line 4 diesel and 1.8 in-line 4 gasoline also offered) |
| Power | 99 kW (133 bhp) @ 4000 rpm |
| Torque | 320 Nm (236 lb. ft) @ 2000 rpm |
| Gearbox | 6-speed manual |
| Installation | Front-engined/front-wheel drive |
| Front suspension | MacPherson strut |
| Rear suspension | Control blade |
| Brakes front/rear | Discs/discs |
| Front tires | 205/55R16 |
| Rear tires | 205/55R16 |
| 0–100 km/h (62 mph) | 9.6 sec |
| Fuel consumption | 5.7 ltr/100 km (41.3 mpg) |
| $CO_2$ emissions | 152 g/km |

*The Car Design Yearbook* normally features only completely new models, but this year we thought it important to include the Focus C-Max, a new derivative of the Ford Focus, because it has been long awaited as a "missing model" in Ford's lineup. It fits into the Ford range between the Fusion and the Galaxy MPV. These models, together with the Maverick and the Tourneo, give Ford a comprehensive range of spacious people-movers.

The Focus C-Max is a mini-MPV and was first revealed at the 2002 Paris Motor Show as a more spacious and versatile Focus concept. Now Ford has finally caught up with Renault in this growing sector by offering this alternative to the new Scénic 2 (see p. 206). The C-Max, however, doesn't stray far from the existing Focus design language. It uses solid character lines on taut surfaces to give restrained emotion, a bit like the Audi A2, but does so in a more approachable fashion than its French direct competitor.

A character line divides the side and top surfaces of the car, giving the roofline and back windows a sleek, sporty look. The side window is recessed into the body-side panel to ensure that the small "catwalk" is maintained right through to the rear, for a satisfyingly solid appearance.

To reduce wind noise and improve fuel economy, aerodynamic drag has been minimized by the use of a number of detailed exterior features, including sleek mirrors and gently protruding wheel arches.

This is a product to watch.

# Ford Freestar

| | |
|---|---|
| Design | Larry Erickson |
| Engine | 4.2 V6 (3.9 V6 also offered) |
| Power | 150 kW (201 bhp) @ 4250 rpm |
| Torque | 360 Nm (265 lb. ft) @ 3500 rpm |
| Gearbox | 4-speed automatic |
| Installation | Front-engined/front-wheel drive |
| Front suspension | MacPherson strut |
| Rear suspension | Twist beam |
| Brakes front/rear | Discs/discs, ABS, EBD |
| Front tires | P235/60R16 |
| Rear tires | P235/60R16 |
| Length | 5105 mm (201 in.) |
| Width | 1946 mm (76.6 in.) |
| Height | 1745 mm (68.7 in.) |
| Wheelbase | 3068 mm (120.8 in.) |
| Track front/rear | 1633/1600 mm (64.3/63 in.) |
| Kerb weight | 1999 kg (4406 lb.) |

Ford's new minivan, the Freestar, combines 4.2-liter V6 performance with the practicalities demanded of this market segment. For, in a minivan more than in any other type of car, form must follow function, and the packaging requirements—the demands of the internal geometry and the positioning of components—define the shape of the exterior very closely. Unfortunately for aesthetes, there's very little scope for application of Ford's favored design language—taut surfaces to create emotion—to the solid block surfaces of a minivan.

The Freestar does, however, sport a stronger stance and proportions than Ford minivans of the past, such as the Aerostar and the Windstar. Large, upright headlights and grille integrate confidently with the hood and front wings for a bold, distinctive, Ford-family look. A short front overhang and an upright nose, combined with integrated body-side cladding, visibly reduce the height and give an athletic proportion. The V6 engine package certainly imposes constraints, but much cleaner lines could have been achieved if the A-pillar had been pushed forward to give a real monospace. Contoured rear bumpers provide a low lift-over height and flow neatly into the one-piece tailgate and tail lights.

With extra investment in interior design, Ford has focused its energies on the cabin environment. The Freestar has an all-new instrument panel divided by wood appliqué in some models, with a two-tone color design between the upper and lower sections of the instrument panel and door trims.

Practicality is the Freestar's main purpose: it can seat up to seven, or for maximum space the third-row seats can be stowed in the floor and the second row removed. The passenger area then turns into a large van offering enough space in the cargo bay to take standard-sized sheets of work materials such as plasterboard or plywood. This adaptability makes it the ideal car for the self-employed man who devotes any spare time he might have to his large family. There are plenty of those around, so the Freestar, nondescript though it is, will no doubt succeed.

# Ford Freestyle FX

| Design | Scott Strong |
|---|---|
| Engine | 3.0 V6 |
| Gearbox | Automatic CVT |
| Installation | Front-engined/all-wheel drive |
| Wheelbase | 2896 mm (114 in.) |

The Freestyle FX is due to make its production debut in 2004, and Ford promises it will unite the rugged looks of an SUV with the driving dynamics and refinement of a sedan, and the security inherent in all-wheel drive.

Featuring an all-new architecture with unitary body construction that crosses over between SUV and pickup, the Freestyle FX has no need for a separate structural frame of the kind many SUVs have, because the supporting structure for the powertrain and suspension are designed into the body parts. Other examples of this idea are the new Range Rover and the BMW X5.

The exterior design is functional rather than emotional but uses many classic Ford design touches, linking this model to the rest of the range. The roof profile sits lower than on an SUV to give the car more of a sedan-like silhouette. However, the body is raised, and fitted low down with aluminum shields, to give it protection during off-road use.

The main area of interest in the Freestyle FX is the roof. At the touch of a button it and the pillars drop away, transforming the vehicle from an SUV into a pickup complete with cargo bed.

The clean look at the front is helped by the headlights, which have integral turn signals. Integrated driving lights sit at opposite ends of the bar that horizontally intersects the air intake in the front bumper.

Large tail lights, complete with LED lights, wrap around the rear wings to provide excellent visibility from the back and sides of the car. The rear tailgate opens downward in a traditional fashion, while the rear screen can be opened up independently of it.

The Freestyle FX is not very exciting to look at, but the functionality of the rear roof arrangement will make it a practical choice for many.

# Ford Model U

It's doubtful that a quantum leap in popular cars as large as that made by the Ford Model T in 1908 could ever occur again, but Ford thinks the Model U is just as visionary. This is a design exploration for a car that is likely to hit the road a hundred years after the immortal "Tin Lizzie" made its debut. Whether or not you concur with such a grand design gesture, the Model U is certainly one of the most innovative concepts launched in 2003.

The Model U concept doesn't just explore user-functionality; it also considers its own effect on global resources by looking at modular design, recyclable materials, emissions, and disassembly.

The exterior three-box profile is tough yet funky, much more successful than the Freestyle concept, but perhaps not the right product just yet for a Ford customer, who may not be ready for anything quite so radical.

The body panels have different finishes and are made of different recyclable materials. The body side is glossy, yet the doors are matt, with grooves to make them appear more structural. The body structure is aluminum and the front side panels are made of a natural fiber-filled composite.

There are many innovations, but the supercharged hydrogen internal-combustion engine is a real world first, although it has not yet been independently validated. The interior is modular, so it can be upgraded as the owner chooses. Also inside, a conversational speech interface allows a person to speak to operate onboard systems, including entertainment, navigation, cellular telephone, and climate control. Pre-crash sensing, adaptive front headlights, and a night-vision system help the driver to avoid accidents.

Advanced materials are designed for their ecological effects and can go from cradle to cradle, instead of staying in the cradle-to-grave waste streams typical of the car industry. Rubber tires use corn-based fillers as a partial substitute for carbon black.

Such innovations are fundamental to the progression of design. In the absence of tougher legislation, more V8-powered trucks will find their way to the marketplace without really challenging designers and engineers to come up with solutions like those embodied in the Model U.

| | |
|---|---|
| Design | Laurens van den Acker |
| Engine | 2.3 in-line 4 hydrogen-powered |
| Power | 113 kW (152 bhp) @ 4500 rpm |
| Torque | 210 Nm (155 lb. ft) @ 4000 rpm |
| Brakes | Discs/discs |
| Length | 4230 mm (166.5 in.) |
| Width | 1810 mm (71.3 in.) |
| Height | 1651 mm (65 in.) |
| Wheelbase | 2685 mm (105.7 in.) |
| Track front/rear | 1583/1583 mm (62.3/62.3 in.) |
| Fuel consumption | 5.2 ltr/100 km (45 mpg) |
| $CO_2$ emissions | PZEV |

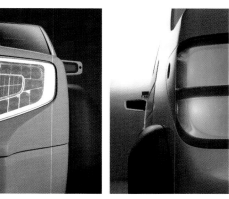

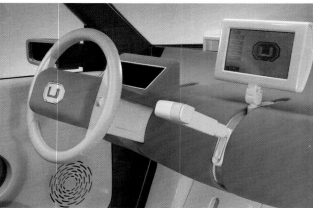

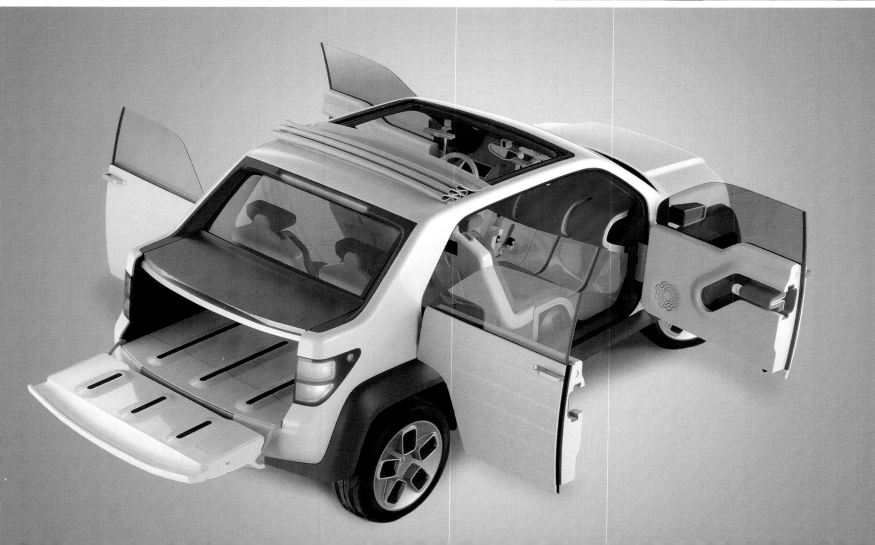

# Ford Mustang GT

| Design | J. Mays and Richard Hutting |
| --- | --- |
| Engine | 4.6 V8 supercharged |
| Power | 298 kW (400 bhp) @ 6000 rpm |
| Torque | 529 Nm (390 lb. ft) @ 3500 rpm |
| Gearbox | 6-speed manual |
| Installation | Front-engined/rear-wheel drive |
| Brakes front/rear | Discs/discs |
| Front tires | 245/40ZR20 |
| Rear tires | 275/35ZR20 |

Forty years after the original Mustang made its world debut and took the market by storm by becoming the fastest-selling car ever (418,000 in 1964, one million by 1966), a further evolution of the famous "pony" car makes its debut in both coupé and convertible concept form. The classic design elements remain: a long hood, a short trunk lid, C-shaped air-scoops behind the doors, and, of course, the grille with its galloping horse, this last item leaving you in no doubt about what model of car this is.

A Mustang for the twenty-first century requires a modern design, though, and taut surfaces and high-tech hardware are evident. The headlights, for example, can zoom in and out using fiber optics and two concentric rings that are shielded behind a single lens.

This car has the Mustang's usual dynamic poise, with its shark-like headlight eyebrows, dramatic hood scoops, and a high waistline. Continuity from front to rear comes from a deep feature line that runs horizontally from the front wheel arch and along the sill and sets up the definition of the main air-scoop. At the rear the tail lights dominate, crossing most of the car. Forward-facing LED projection lights, offset against a parabola, use precision mirrors to help to minimize hotspots.

The contemporary interior is awash with bright red and contrasting charcoal leather, and accented with aluminum highlights for a pseudo-technical finish. A circular theme is used throughout. The instrument bezels have sprocket gears rather than needle pointers; they feature a gear-driven trolley, scored with indicator lines, that rides around the inside of the bezel to display the revs and road speed.

There is no denying that Ford's new Mustang GT concept celebrates its heritage to the full. Let's hope Ford is brave enough to launch such a contemporary interior design.

# Ford Streetka

| | |
|---|---|
| Design | David Wilkie |
| Engine | 1.6 in-line 4 |
| Power | 70 kW (94 bhp) @ 5500 rpm |
| Torque | 135 Nm (99 lb. ft) @ 4250 rpm |
| Gearbox | 5-speed manual |
| Installation | Front-engined/front-wheel drive |
| Front suspension | MacPherson strut |
| Rear suspension | Twist beam |
| Brakes front/rear | Discs/drums |
| Front tires | 195/45R16 |
| Rear tires | 195/45R16 |
| Length | 3650 mm (143.7 in.) |
| Width | 1695 mm (66.7 in.) |
| Height | 1335 mm (52.6 in.) |
| Wheelbase | 2448 mm (96.4 in.) |
| Track front/rear | 1417/1452 mm (55.8/57.2 in.) |
| Curb weight | 1061 kg (2339 lb.) |
| 0–100 km/h (62 mph) | 12.1 sec |
| Top speed | 173 km/h (108 mph) |
| Fuel consumption | 7.9 ltr/100 km (29.8 mpg) |
| $CO_2$ emissions | 190 g/km |

The Streetka has been eagerly awaited since the concept for it was first unveiled at the Turin Motor Show in 2000. The original, racy-looking design—christened Saetta—was designed by Ghia, Ford's venerable design house in Turin, which since then has virtually closed down. It featured a radically sporty exterior and a cockpit bursting with bright aluminum and red fabric.

The production model has been slightly tamed. Designed for production, and built by Pininfarina in Italy, the latest Streetka broadly retains the concept's exterior style. At the front, the edgy design translates into sharp new headlights, while the rear has new lights that triangulate downward, eventually meeting the single exhaust pipe in the center. The result is a customer-ready model that is less overtly a Ka, yet still distinctly recognizable as one thanks to its blistered wheel arches and rounded profiles. The concept's interior, however—and alas—has been substantially toned down to a more conventional Ka one, no doubt to reduce project costs.

The Streetka is aimed at fashion-conscious, pop-music-addicted twenty- and thirty-somethings. With that in mind, Ford has recruited Kylie Minogue to promote the car, which gives you an idea of where the Streetka brand is heading.

Surprisingly, the Streetka is the smallest convertible yet produced by Ford, although it is not the first Ford to be built in Italy: in the early 1960s an Italian-assembled and restyled version of the Ford Anglia 105E, called the Anglia Torino, was built. If only Ford had predicted the Streetka's rapturous reception— it is probably kicking itself for not getting it to market faster, when the Ka itself was still fresh out of the box. Still, the rub-off will surely strengthen the Ka brand and boost sales of all Ka derivatives.

# GM Hy-wire

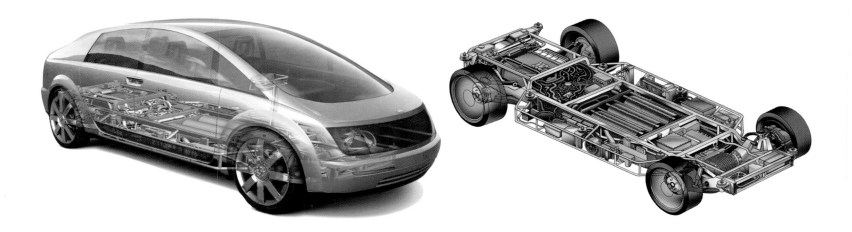

| Design | Ed Welburn |
|---|---|
| Engine | 200 single fuel cells generating 125–200 volts |
| Power | 60 kW (80 bhp) |
| Torque | 216 Nm (159 lb. ft) |
| Installation | Mid-engined/front-wheel drive |
| Front tires | 225/40R20 |
| Rear tires | 245/40R22 |
| Length | 4953 mm (195 in.) |
| Width | 1870 mm (74 in.) |
| Height | 1570 mm (62 in.) |
| Wheelbase | 3114 mm (122.6 in.) |
| Curb weight | 1898 kg (4185 lb.) |
| Top speed | 160 km/h (100 mph) |

The Hy-wire concept is one of the most forward-looking in this book, an evolution of the GM AUTOnomy, which was heaped with praise for its "skateboard" profile and powertrain concept at the North American International Auto Show in 2002.

In addition to keeping that innovative skateboard-shaped chassis, which contains all the propulsion, transmission, steering, and braking components, the Hy-wire adds a practical body on top via ten mechanical connecting points and just a single electrical connection. A key feature is that the skateboard chassis gives the absolute maximum freedom for designing alternative vehicle body architecture for a common chassis.

The Hy-wire uses electrical signals instead of mechanical linkages or hydraulics to operate acceleration, braking, and steering functions. All these major driver-control functions are consolidated into a drive-by-wire system developed by the Swedish firm SKF, resulting in a reduction in weight.

Convention is turned on its head. For instance, the absence of a traditional internal-combustion or electric engine means there is no need for a cooling grille up front. Instead of fitting one, GM has enclosed the front with glass to give the driver a greater view of the road ahead.

The X-Drive control slides to the left or right, depending on which driving side is needed for a given territory. A button starts the vehicle and also engages its forward, reverse and neutral drive conditions.

Cameras have replaced rear-view mirrors, and the headlights and tail lights feature LED technology, so they can be packaged in a small space.

GM, in an illustration of its seriousness about Hy-wire, has filed over thirty patents covering its technologies, its manufacturing processes, and even the business models involved in producing it. This is definitely one concept that won't just vanish into thin air. It certainly isn't the production version, but some day we will see one.

# Honda Accord

| Design | Honda Motor Corporation |
|---|---|
| Engine | 3.0 V6 (2.4 in-line 4 also offered) |
| Power | 179 kW (240 bhp) @ 6250 rpm |
| Torque | 288 Nm (212 lb. ft) @ 5000 rpm |
| Gearbox | 5-speed automatic |
| Installation | Front-engined/front-wheel drive |
| Front suspension | Double wishbone |
| Rear suspension | Double wishbone |
| Brakes front/rear | Discs/discs, ABS, EBD |
| Front tires | 205/60R16 |
| Rear tires | 205/60R16 |
| Length | 4813 mm (189.5 in.) |
| Width | 1816 mm (71.5 in.) |
| Height | 1450 mm (57.1 in.) |
| Wheelbase | 2740 mm (107.9 in.) |
| Track front/rear | 1552/1554mm (61.1/61.2 in.) |
| Curb weight | 1524 kg (3360 lb.) |

It is a privileged job having to redesign the bestselling car in America, but the task must come with a good share of worries. How far to progress the design, to demonstrate it is up to date, while protecting loyal customers and market share? In the USA alone, more than eight million Accords have been sold since the model went on sale in 1976; that is some achievement, but a weighty legacy for designers.

Honda's design center in Japan says that the difference between Japanese and European customer expectations has become much smaller, but the US market still requires larger engines and unique exterior styling. Therefore, cars made for Europe and Japan appear to be identical, but versions made for America are fractionally wider and longer, to accommodate a V6 engine. There is a coupé too, but it is offered only in the USA.

The new model is altogether crisper than its predecessor. The headlights now have sharp outlines and the nose a more chiseled look. The side profile has a high-rising waistline to project strength and sportiness, with an abruptly truncated rear similar to those produced by makes like Alfa Romeo and Audi. Pull door handles and mirror-mounted indicators add to the perception of quality.

Hondas always score highly in the influential JD Power quality surveys in the USA, so, irrespective of how radical the new design was going to be, sales of Honda's new Accord were always certain to be enormous. And the company has managed to add a tiny bit of "edge" to one of the most loyally bought of all cars.

# Honda Element

| | |
|---|---|
| Engine | 2.4 in-line 4 |
| Power | 119 kW (160 bhp) @ 5500 rpm |
| Torque | 218 Nm (161 lb. ft) @ 4500 rpm |
| Gearbox | 5-speed manual or 4-speed automatic |
| Installation | Front-engined/2-wheel drive or 4-wheel drive |
| Front suspension | MacPherson strut |
| Rear suspension | Double wishbone |
| Brakes front/rear | Discs/discs |
| Front tires | 215/70R16 |
| Rear tires | 215/70R16 |
| Length | 4229 mm (166.5 in.) |
| Width | 1816 mm (71.5 in.) |
| Height | 1880 mm (74 in.) |
| Wheelbase | 2576 mm (101.4 in.) |
| Track front/rear | 1577 mm (62.1/62.3 in.) |
| Curb weight | 1521 kg (3352 lb.) |
| Fuel consumption | 10.7 ltr/100 km (22 mpg) |

Development of the Element began in 1998, when a group of young designers and engineers working at Honda's US research group set out to create a car offering the sort of utility that young, active people of Generation Y seek. The first result of their labors was the Model X concept, which took its bow in 2001 at the Detroit International Auto Show. So positive was the feedback that a production version was given the go-ahead, and the Element is the result.

Generation Y is a 71-million-strong swath of new buyers in their late teens and early twenties, who are entering the automotive market with no obvious vehicle to fit their needs. Honda reckons the Element addresses this question, since it is specifically designed for those who surf, snowboard, or mountain-bike.

Key design features are generous interior proportions with good side and rear access, a flat floor with flexible seating that folds flat into a bed or can be removed completely, and a rugged exterior with tough panels. The center-opening, swing-wide doors have no B-pillars, for maximum cargo-loading flexibility.

Inside, the materials are chosen to be easy to clean, scratch-resistant, and waterproof. The use of two-tone colors in blocks gives the Element a product design feel that is, Honda insists, unique and in tune with the Gen-Y buyer. The exterior is fairly square, with not much ornamentation, and the rear section has heavily tinted glass for privacy.

# Hyundai HIC

| | |
|---|---|
| Design | Hyundai's design center in Japan |
| Engine | 3.5 V6 |
| Power | 194 kW (260 bhp) |
| Torque | 299 Nm (220 lb. ft) |
| Front tires | 245/40R20 |
| Rear tires | 245/40R20 |
| Length | 4750 mm (187 in.) |
| Width | 1995 mm (78.5 in.) |
| Height | 1300 mm (56.9 in.) |
| Wheelbase | 2750 mm (108.3 in.) |

Hyundai has enjoyed recent critical and sales success with its characterful Tiburon Coupé. Its concept cars, however, sometimes fall wide of the mark—for instance, the Clix, featured in *The Car Design Yearbook 1*, was hardly a memorable piece of automotive thinking.

Hyundai unveiled the HIC, the so-called High-technology Intelligence Coupé, concept at the 2002 Seoul Motor Show. It was styled at Hyundai's Japanese design center and is a low-slung two-plus-two. As such, it has quite a satisfying shape but, to make it more striking, Hyundai has used two-tone paintwork to highlight the gently curving wings and bumper moldings. This has the effect of weighting the corners and making the HIC appear dumpy and flaccid—not helpful for the image of an attention-grabbing coupé.

The HIC concept is really all about Hyundai's new technologies, in particular ones that might later graduate to production models. Included here are an intelligent proximity-sensing cruise control that keeps the car at a constantly safe distance from the vehicle in front, night visibility capabilities, and a CCTV peripheral monitoring system that replaces rear-view mirrors and allows the driver to see completely around the car.

Hyundai is also developing, in collaboration with IBM, a new-generation telematics system. Its focus will be on voice-operated computing services to make driving safer and easier.

It is hard to imagine how the HIC's design DNA will translate to Hyundai's future production models. But then this is not really the point: the HIC is merely a show-stopper to draw attention to the company's trick electronics.

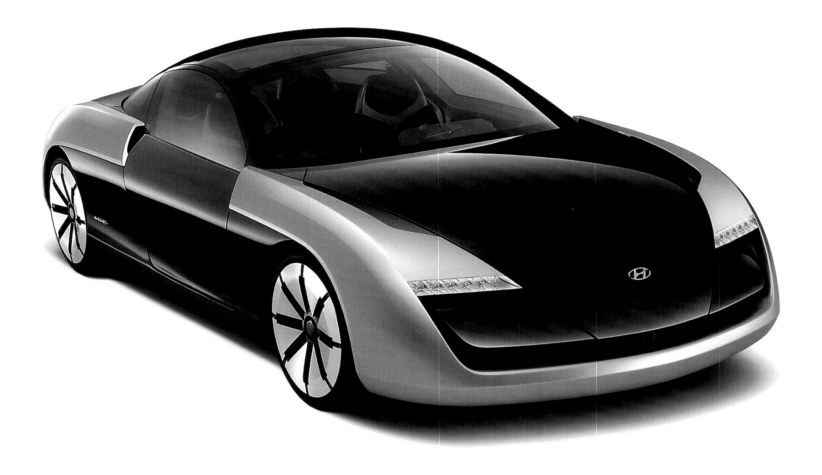

# Infiniti FX45

The FX45 is the fourth all-new Infiniti introduced in less than twelve months, and follows the G35 Sport Sedan, the G35 Sport Coupé, and the M45 performance sedan to give Infiniti a fresh, new range that some rival manufacturers can only dream of.

A distinctly curvaceous SUV, with more of a "car-like" persona than a go-anywhere truck look, the FX45 blends an SUV lower body with a sleek upper body reminiscent of a sports car.

The FX45 has a strong, purposeful stance, a long, sleek hood, and an arched upper body, this last form being reflected in its curved doors, tailgate, hood, and bumpers. Taut and elegant surfaces give a rather friendly look to a car that packs either V6 or predatory V8 power. The headlights and tail lights are relatively small by SUV standards, also imbuing the FX45 with a more car-like appearance.

The five-passenger interior is warm and inviting, with a rich mix of burnt-orange leather and a black instrument panel complete with white switchgear inscriptions. The two-tone color design wraps around the cabin, the surfaces of which, like the exterior, are uncluttered and restful. There is a sense of quality and careful attention to detail, exemplified by both the chrome rims around the instruments and the tightly fitting switchgear.

This is a very successful design that breaks the mold for SUVs. Definitely more stylish than the Porsche Cayenne and many other, less starry alternatives, it's sure to be a hit.

And for those non-US readers who might be wondering, Infiniti is the premium Nissan brand; the brand names are related in the same way that Lexus relates to Toyota.

| | |
|---|---|
| Engine | 4.5 V8 (3.5 V6 also offered) |
| Power | 235 kW (315 bhp) |
| Gearbox | 5-speed automatic |
| Installation | Front-engined/all-wheel drive |
| Front suspension | MacPherson strut |
| Rear suspension | Multi-link |
| Brakes front/rear | Discs/discs, BA, EBD |
| Front tires | 265/50R20 |
| Rear tires | 265/50R20 |
| Wheelbase | 2850 mm (112.2 in.) |
| Track front/rear | 1593/1641 mm (62.7/64.6 in.) |
| Fuel consumption | 12.4 ltr/100 km (19mpg) |

# Infiniti M45

| | |
|---|---|
| Engine | 4.5 V8 |
| Power | 254 kW (340 bhp) @ 6400 rpm |
| Torque | 452 Nm (333 lb. ft) @ 4000 rpm |
| Gearbox | 5-speed automatic |
| Installation | Front-engined/rear-wheel drive |
| Front suspension | MacPherson strut |
| Rear suspension | Multi-link |
| Brakes front/rear | Discs/discs TCS, BA, EBD |
| Front tires | 235/45R18 |
| Rear tires | 235/45R18 |
| Length | 5009 mm (197.2 in.) |
| Width | 1770 mm (69.7 in.) |
| Height | 1463 mm (57.6 in.) |
| Wheelbase | 2799 mm (110.2 in.) |
| Track front/rear | 1509/1509 mm (59.4/59.4 in.) |
| Curb weight | 1747 kg (3851 lb.) |
| Fuel consumption | 11.8 ltr/100 km (19.9 mpg) |

The all-new V8-powered Infiniti M45 is positioned between Nissan's flagship Q45 and the new Infiniti G35 Sport Sedan.

Infiniti is the manufacturer's premium brand, tilted at a primarily US customer base. Unlike Nissan, which now has a strong product character with the new Primera and Micra, thanks to input from Renault's head of design, Patrick le Quément (Renault is Nissan's majority shareholder), Infiniti has stuck to its conservative and inoffensive guns. There is nothing wrong with the M45's understated exterior, but it suggests a comfortable cruising car rather than an outright performer with V8 firepower in its belly. It is cautious where a Mercedes-Benz S-Class exudes excitement.

The M45 has a more squared-off appearance than the smaller G35. Its front end is dominated by an aggressive front grille, with wide, black-chrome horizontal bars that flow into the moderately sporty xenon headlights. Viewed from the side, the silhouette is a wedge shape running from front to rear, with a swept-back C-pillar and a steeply running-off trunk that contrasts with an upright A-pillar.

Inside, the contoured front seats are finished with "Sojourner" leather exclusive to the Infiniti brand. The interior also features a bird's-eye-maple trim with a smoked-graphite color, and a performance-oriented four-dial instrument cluster complete with amber lighting that silhouettes the gauges.

Progressive technology is strongly featured, too. There is a vehicle information system consisting of a large, multifunction LCD screen and an optional DVD-based navigation system, an intelligent cruise control that maintains driver-selected following distances, and the Infiniti voice-recognition system shared with the Q45.

The M45 is a dignified and technically accomplished luxury car, then, but a bit of an identity-free zone.

# Infiniti Triant

| | |
|---|---|
| Engine | 3.5 V6 |
| Gearbox | 5-speed automatic |
| Installation | Front-engined/all-wheel drive |
| Front tires | 255/55R19 |
| Rear tires | 255/55R19 |

The Triant concept is really a future design study, but it would, nevertheless, easily fit into Infiniti's existing range right now. It's a muscular coupé/SUV, with a cab-rearward design and Japanese crafted surfaces. It has some head-turning features, most notably the gullwing doors, over 1.65 meters (5.5 ft) long and opening to nearly 2.15 meters (7 ft) in height.

The Infiniti grille sits between two rising headlights that give the Triant a grimacing visage. The headlights continue up on to the wing ridges to join a line that runs out at the base of the windshield. Lower down on the wing, a feature begins and extends rearward, creating a shelf that eventually wraps over on to the rear lights.

The headlights are controlled by GPS; the high beam swings up to fifteen degrees, while the low beam swings up to thirty degrees on corners, improving night visibility, especially on twisty roads.

The interior design is a work of art. Red and black organic and eye-catching surfaces adorn the cabin. Complex forms drape over the instrument panel, door panels, and rear seat, creating a striking but harmonious environment. A sweeping center console runs from the instrument panel down between the seats, visually connecting the front and rear areas.

Driver and passenger seats are mounted on shock absorbers, similar in design to active engine mounts and also found on modern lifeboat seats. The seats react to different driving situations, and alter the driving height and damping levels to best suit the driving style and terrain.

# Invicta S1

| | |
|---|---|
| Design | Leigh Adams |
| Engine | 4.6 V8 |
| Power | 239 kW (320 bhp) @ 5900 rpm |
| Torque | 407 Nm (300 lb. ft) @ 4800 rpm |
| Gearbox | 5-speed manual |
| Installation | Front-engined/rear-wheel drive |
| Front suspension | Double wishbone |
| Rear suspension | Double wishbone |
| Brakes front/rear | Discs/discs |
| Front tires | 255/35ZR19 |
| Rear tires | 275/35ZR19 |
| Length | 4400 mm (173.2 in.) |
| Width | 2000 mm (78.7 in.) |
| Height | 1225 mm (48.2 in.) |
| Wheelbase | 2500 mm (98.4 in.) |
| Track front/rear | 1780/1730 mm (70.1/68.1 in.) |
| Curb weight | 1098 kg (2420 lb.) |
| 0–100 km/h (62 mph) | 5 sec |
| Top speed | 274 km/h (170 mph) |
| Fuel consumption | 11.3 ltr/100 km (20.8 mpg) |

Invicta is a revival of a make that has not been represented in the price lists since 1950, and whose heyday was a good fifteen years before that. Moreover, a resurrection of the name (which comes from the White Knight of Edmund Spenser's late sixteenth-century allegorical romance *The Faerie Queene*) has been attempted several times in the intervening period.

The first Invicta of modern times, therefore, should be an intriguing confection. And the new Invicta Car Company has harnessed the design ethos of the original prewar designers like Reid Railton and William Watson, who ensured that every component projected a masculine message of speed, power, and visual drama.

A high waistline and a low overall height combine to give a somewhat cocooned and secure feeling inside the S1. The interior is sumptuous, with wall-to-wall tan and gray leather, and metallic detailing on instruments, center console, and pedals.

Outside, the Invicta winged badge straddles the inset hood and "smiling" grille, while the front apron drops at the edges to give more coverage to the front wheels. This feature of dropped skirting is mirrored at the sides, on the sills, and on the rear apron.

In the 1930s Invictas were robustly engineered, with a quality that closely matched Rolls-Royce, and engines that gave enormous torque outputs. The S1's construction, though, is unique: it is the world's first production car with a one-piece carbon-fiber bodyshell. This is bonded to a steel tubular spaceframe chassis to create a very strong, stiff, and lightweight structure that gives high torsional rigidity for good roadholding and excellent occupant-cell integrity for enhanced safety. With power from Ford's V8 Mustang engine, the S1 promises to be rapid, safe, and stylish—something Invicta's founder, Noel Macklin, would be proud of.

Of course, the S1 faces tough competition from prestige makes like Porsche and Maserati. But, hopefully, for the sake of automotive biodiversity, it will rekindle this vintage name while bringing exciting motoring to an exclusive coterie of owners.

# Italdesign Moray

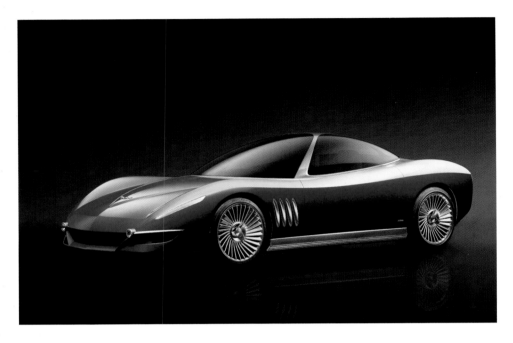

| | |
|---|---|
| Design | Italdesign |
| Engine | 6.0 V8 |
| Power | 298 kW (400 bhp) @ 6500 rpm |
| Gearbox | 4-speed automatic |
| Installation | Front-engined/rear-wheel drive |
| Brakes front/rear | Discs/discs |
| Front tires | 255/35ZR20 |
| Rear tires | 335/30ZR20 |
| Length | 4540 mm (178.7 in.) |
| Width | 1950 mm (76.8 in.) |
| Height | 1235 mm (48.6 in.) |
| Track front/rear | 1660/1575 mm (65.4/62 in.) |

The Moray is an Italian-led project by Giorgetto Giugiaro and his son Fabrizio, of Italdesign, to celebrate fifty years of the Chevrolet Corvette, that iconic and evergreen symbol of the American sports car. Based on current Corvette mechanicals, this sleek coupé concept can be transformed into a roadster simply by removing the clear, domed roof.

The name comes from the Moray eel, found in the Mediterranean, and the organic design language sums up this creature. The car's slender body is constructed primarily of a single contour line that rises from the low serpentine hood, with its long and slender front lights. The front and rear have sharp, angular features that contrast with the flowing surfaces of the side profile. Another highly striking feature is the thirty-spoke turbine wheels, which also contrast with the relatively uninterrupted body side.

Lower down, aluminum sill protectors visually link the wheels. The bluff rear end houses the obligatory Corvette four circular stop lights, and also has a rear underbody guard that helps continuity at the sides. There are no side mirrors, these having been replaced by a camera system with dashboard-integrated viewers. Inside, the upholstery is of soft leather.

What are the design objectives of this exercise? Neither Chevrolet nor Italdesign is saying. But we can assume it's a great way for the Italian house to salute its relationship with General Motors, and Chevrolet in particular. Whatever the motivation, this is an excellent object lesson in how to combine curvaceous surfaces with detailed features and still achieve a balanced look.

# Jaguar XJ

| Design | Ian Callum |
|---|---|
| Engine | 4.2 V8 (3.0 V6 and 3.5 V8 also offered) |
| Power | 298 kW (400 bhp) @ 6100 rpm |
| Torque | 553 Nm (408 lb. ft) @ 3500 rpm |
| Gearbox | 6-speed automatic |
| Installation | Front-engined/rear-wheel drive |
| Front suspension | Double wishbone |
| Rear suspension | Double wishbone |
| Brakes front/rear | Discs/discs |
| Front tires | 255/40R19 |
| Rear tires | 255/40R19 |
| Length | 5080 mm (200 in.) |
| Width | 1868 mm (73.5 in.) |
| Height | 1448 mm (57 in.) |
| Wheelbase | 3034 mm (119.4 in.) |
| Track front/rear | 1556/1546 mm (61.3/60.9 in.) |
| Kerb weight | 1665 kg (3671 lb.) |
| 0–100 km/h (62 mph) | 5.3 sec |
| Top speed | 249 km/h (155 mph) |
| Fuel consumption | 12.3 ltr/100 km (19.1 mpg) |
| $CO_2$ emissions | 299 g/km |

This new XJ from Jaguar is the seventh generation of its flagship sedan, first introduced in 1968. While in many ways a subtle evolution of thirty-four years of timelessness, it is also the most radical rendition to date—on the inside.

It is longer, taller, and wider than its predecessor, giving more interior room, although the iconic shape remains largely the same. Subtle changes include deeper doors, a higher waistline, and a marginally more "cab-forward" package; the front overhang is reduced and the windshield rake is faster, but the smaller hood still retains the characteristically sculpted XJ shape, initiated from the oval headlights. The headlights are set either side of a new grille, with intersecting vertical and horizontal bars, which takes its inspiration from the original 1968 model.

As with all XJs in the past, the latest technology features strongly, but the most advanced new feature is a choice of material. The body is made from riveted and bonded aluminum, resulting in a body-weight reduction of around 40% and shaving a hefty 200 kg (441 lb.) off the complete car.

The interior styling uses gently curved surfaces and quality materials to give the kind of comfortable, executive atmosphere you would expect from a top-of-the-range Jaguar. The sporty versions have a combination of charcoal dashboard and gray-stained bird's-eye-maple veneer, while classic models have traditional burr-walnut finish. A new option is piano-black trim, a highly polished finish used on the center console and gearshift surround.

Inside, another new technology enhances safety: JaguarVoice is the voice-activated control of the audio system, telephone, climate control, and navigation.

# Kia KCD-1 Slice

A new crossover car from Kia, the Slice concept is a sporty design that can carry up to six people. According to Kia, the theme from the outset was that all non-essential features should be excised—hence the name Slice.

The faired-in headlights, and the narrow grille with orange trim flanking the Kia badge, give the Slice a striking, youthful look. A view from the side reveals a strong feature line that links the front wheel arch to the rear one. The "fast" windshield stretches in a single arc up on to the roof, where it continues until the roof kicks up over the rear hatch to give a sporty flourish.

Other exterior features include the tapered indentation above the sills and bold, dish-type wheels that emphasize the Slice's performance and rugged capabilities. At the rear are high-mounted tail lights that wrap around the C-pillars, orange-accented bumpers, and curved rear glass. The doors are solenoid-operated and have no B-pillars. Small push-button door openers are located in the window frames. The front doors are conventionally hinged, while the rear doors are hinged behind to provide completely accessible space when both are open.

The dashboard follows the Slice color scheme in being topped with a splash of bright orange. In its center is a control interface that offers big push-buttons for the most frequently used controls, and a pop-up LCD screen for navigation, information, or entertainment displays.

No production plans have been announced for the Slice; that seems to be completely normal for Kia's concept cars, which are always more adventurous than its humdrum showroom fare. Still, it will complete the motor-show circuit in 2003, where it's sure to add a dash of color. Orange, to be precise.

| Design | Eric Stoddard |
|---|---|
| Engine | 2.7 V6 |
| Gearbox | Sportmatic manual or auto |
| Installation | Front-engined/all-wheel drive |
| Front suspension | Double wishbone |
| Rear suspension | Multi-link |
| Front tires | 235/45R19 |
| Rear tires | 235/45R19 |
| Length | 4496 mm (177 in.) |
| Width | 1829 mm (72 in.) |
| Height | 1600 mm (63 in.) |
| Wheelbase | 2845 mm (112 in.) |

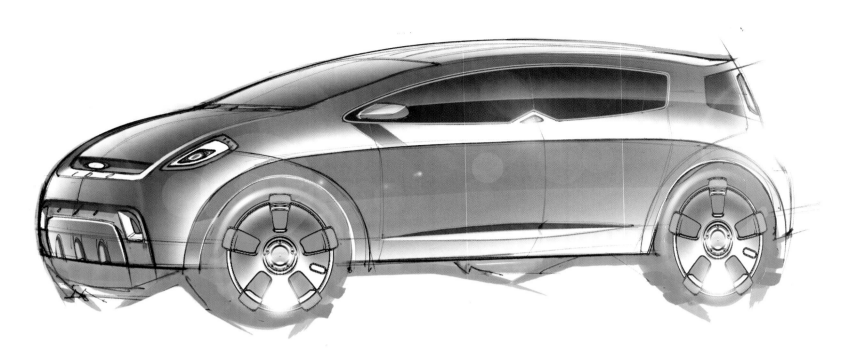

STODDARD

# Kia KCV-II

| Design | Jay Baek and Peter Arcardipane |
|---|---|
| Engine | 3.5 V6 |
| Torque | 294 Nm (217 lb. ft) @ 3000 rpm |
| Gearbox | 5-speed automatic |
| Installation | Front-engined/4-wheel drive |
| Front suspension | MacPherson strut |
| Rear suspension | Strut with trailing arm |
| Brakes front/rear | Discs/discs |
| Front tires | 255/50R20 |
| Rear tires | 255/50R20 |
| Length | 4535 mm (178.5 in.) |
| Width | 1860 mm (73.2 in.) |
| Height | 1820 mm (71.7 in.) |
| Wheelbase | 2615 mm (103 in.) |
| Track front/rear | 1590/1660 mm (62.6/65.4 in.) |
| Kerb weight | 1620 kg (3571 lb.) |
| 0–100 km/h (62 mph) | 8.5 sec |
| Top speed | 210 km/h (130 mph) |

A funky new crossover concept from Kia, the KCV-II is intended to drum up some new excitement for this sometimes lackluster brand by targeting youthful car owners who enjoy an active lifestyle. Kia says the target audience is the "bobo" generation, which stands for "bourgeois bohemians." These are, we are told, people who are economically bourgeois but spiritually bohemian—a mixture of 1960s hippies and 1980s yuppies.

The KCV-II has an all-new platform designed so that it can accommodate several body styles, from a conventional sports utility vehicle to a lifestyle variant like the KCV-II concept that Kia has come up with. With high ground clearance, a commanding driving position, and an open pickup cargo space, the KCV-II has the stance and tough looks of an SUV.

The body's curvaceous surfaces make it look softer, in an effort to target female bobos. Non-automotive products have been used for inspiration throughout: design elements from motorcycles, furniture, architecture, and consumer products are fused together here.

A striking feature is the aluminum band that circles the car, starting at the nose, running along the waist, and finishing as a guardrail over the pickup bed. This highlights the wedge of the profile—a classic styling feature used to imply dynamism in a car's look.

The KCV-II's "scissor" doors would more usually be found on a Lamborghini—the Countach, Diablo, or Murciélago—as well as on Toyota's short-lived 1990s Sera, and, unsurprisingly, give a sporty feel to the body architecture. They also have the practical effect of improving access to the rear seats.

The interior has a warm mix of pastel leather shades and precision-machined surfaces. Instruments are clustered around the steering column, their design inspired by motorcycle instrument binnacles.

For those in the back, the rear glass windshield hinges upward so that when the rear seats are reclined the passengers are partly exposed to the elements, just as in a cabriolet.

# Lamborghini Gallardo

| Design | Lamborghini Centro Stile |
|---|---|
| Engine | 5.0 V10 |
| Power | 373 kW (500 bhp) @ 7800 rpm |
| Torque | 510 Nm (376 lb. ft) @ 4500 rpm |
| Gearbox | 6-speed manual |
| Installation | Mid-rear-engined/4-wheel drive |
| Front suspension | Double wishbone |
| Rear suspension | Double wishbone |
| Brakes front/rear | Discs/discs |
| Front tires | 235/35R19 |
| Rear tires | 295/30R19 |
| Length | 4300 mm (169.3 in.) |
| Width | 1900 mm (74.8 in.) |
| Height | 1165 mm (45.9 in.) |
| Wheelbase | 2560 mm (100.8 in.) |
| Track front/rear | 1622/1592 mm (63.9/62.7 in.) |
| Kerb weight | 1430 kg (3153 lb.) |
| Top speed | 290 km/h (180 mph) |

For anyone in the market for a car like a Porsche 911 Turbo, it could be a very special Christmas this year. Lamborghini has just launched the beautiful Gallardo, an all-new offering that will bring the famous Italian make within the reach of previously excluded customers. This car is still not cheap, at an expected price of 200,000 euros, but it does, at last, give Lamborghini a sports model that Porsche buyers can seriously consider.

Following the tradition started by founder Ferruccio Lamborghini with the Miura, the Gallardo takes its name from a breed of fighting bull. The Gallardo stock, one of the five main breeds of such bulls, became famous in the eighteenth century for its aggressive beauty and domineering strength. And, so you don't disgrace yourself in Lamborghini circles, it's pronounced "Ga-yardo."

The car's flowing waistline has more in common with today's Ferraris than with the rather angular lines of past Lamborghinis. The Gallardo has conventional opening doors rather than the more complex, scissors-style arrangement that began with the 1972 Countach and continues today in the Murciélago; such doors are now reserved for the models in the make's twelve-cylinder lineage. However, the angular front and rear features of the Murciélago are carried over here.

Even though this compact, two-seater junior supercar is significantly cheaper than the Murciélago, you still get awesome Lamborghini presence, and a V10 engine with 373 kW (500 bhp) of power that can propel you beyond 290 km/h (180 mph). So regular Lamborghini aficionados are sure to love it. Under Volkswagen ownership, makes like Lamborghini and Bentley are being given the investment to go after larger markets, but the vast majority of us who still can't afford a Gallardo shouldn't expect Lamborghini to introduce anything more populist than this.

# Lancia Ypsilon

The new Ypsilon was inspired by the 1950s Lancia Ardea sedan, itself a development of the advanced Aprilia small car introduced in 1936. However, this car is essentially an evolution of the former Ypsilon model, and while it has a much more solid stance than its forebear, it retains its femininity.

The large vertical grille that sits between the fingernail-shaped headlights, now with clear lenses, dominates the front end. The Lancia grille is highly distinctive—a real plus because so many cars strive to have such a strong visual identity but have no heritage to draw on. By contrast, Lancia was founded ninety-seven years ago.

Along the sides, a strongly defined horizontal beltline, together with a styling motif, runs the length of the car, over the wheel arches, to form a link between front and rear. Lines at the rear end converge on a single imaginary focal point situated low down behind the bumper, helping to make the car look well grounded. The beltline drops at the rear and retains the design cue from the old Ypsilon, but instead of "kissing" the wheel arches as before, it's now higher up, to provide a more solid look.

At the rear, tall, upright taillights enclose the tailgate and follow the style of the contemporary Lancia Thesis with a vertical theme, edged in chrome. Chrome is also used to highlight the grille surround, door handles, emblems, and rear number-plate plinth. All that glittering metal reinforces the upmarket effect.

The interior is also an evolution of the last one, which was launched in 1998. The center-mounted instruments remain but are now ringed in chrome and come with more traditional markings. The colors and materials are characteristically Lancia, with leather and Alcantara used throughout in high-contrast color combinations.

Lancias are unmistakably and unashamedly Italian in their execution. Sales of this brand have been declining for years, however. Could these two facts be connected?

| | |
|---|---|
| Design | Flavio Manzoni |
| Engine | 1.3 diesel |
| Length | 3760 mm (148 in.) |
| Width | 1690 mm (66.5 in.) |
| Wheelbase | 2390 mm (94.1 in.) |

# Lexus RX330

| | |
|---|---|
| Engine | 3.3 V6 |
| Power | 172 kW (230 bhp) @ 5600 rpm |
| Torque | 328 Nm (242 lb. ft) @ 3600 rpm |
| Gearbox | 5-speed automatic |
| Installation | Front-engined/front-wheel drive |
| Front suspension | MacPherson strut |
| Rear suspension | Dual-link strut |
| Brakes front/rear | Discs/discs |
| Front tires | 225/65R17 |
| Rear tires | 225/65R17 |
| Length | 4729 mm (186.2 in.) |
| Width | 1844 mm (72.6 in.) |
| Height | 1679 mm (66.1 in.) |
| Wheelbase | 2715 mm (106.9 in.) |
| Track front/rear | 1575/1554 mm (62.0/61.2 in.) |
| Curb weight | 1751 kg (3860 lb.) |
| 0–100 km/h (62 mph) | 7.7 sec |
| Top speed | 180 km/h (112 mph) |
| Fuel consumption | 10.9 ltr/100 km (21.6 mpg) |

Slightly larger than the RX300 model it replaces, the new RX330 is the curvaceous luxury SUV from Lexus that is now the brand's contender in the entry-level luxury SUV class. It forms part of a three-series SUV strategy by Lexus that also includes the new GX470, a V8-powered SUV positioned between the RX330 and the premium-luxury LX470. This wide choice reflects the fact that the very important and highly lucrative SUV market is still expanding not only in the USA but in Europe too.

The RX330 is in head-on battle with the Infiniti FX45. They both have exterior design that is more "car-like" in profile, with a curved roof, a "fast" windshield, and an angled rear screen and C-pillars. The RX330, however, has higher ground clearance. The style is certainly less aggressive than that of most other larger and more rugged SUVs.

It's the equipment and technology, however, that warrant most discussion: the rear seats offer sliding and reclining adjustments; the tailgate is available as a powered option controlled from the remote entry system; automatic air suspension alters the ride height to suit the terrain and speed, and lowers it to offer easier access; adaptive front lighting helps to illuminate a turn as the driver steers into it; a reversing camera mounted above the rear number plate projects the view on to the navigation screen; and there is an adaptive laser cruise-control system similar to the LS430's.

The Lexus Link system combines GPS satellite and mobile-phone technology to connect the customer with Lexus Link advisors at any time, the only proviso being that the car must be able to receive a cellular signal. Lexus Link includes automatic notification of airbag deployment, dispatch of emergency services, accident assistance, roadside assistance with location, theft notification, and stolen-vehicle tracking, plus remote door locking and unlocking.

Let no one suggest Lexus doesn't furnish its products with gadgetry.

# Lincoln Aviator

| Design | Gerry McGovern |
|---|---|
| Engine | 4.6 V8 |
| Power | 225 kW (302 bhp) @ 5750 rpm |
| Torque | 407 Nm (300 lb. ft) @ 3250 rpm |
| Gearbox | 5-speed automatic |
| Installation | Front-engined/rear-wheel drive or all-wheel drive |
| Front suspension | Independent short and long arm |
| Rear suspension | Independent short and long arm |
| Brakes front/rear | Discs/discs, EBD |
| Front tires | 245/65R17 |
| Rear tires | 245/65R17 |
| Length | 4910 mm (193.3 in.) |
| Width | 1930 mm (76 in.) |
| Height | 1814 mm (71.4 in.) |
| Wheelbase | 2888 mm (113.7 in.) |
| Track front/rear | 1547/1554 mm (60.9/61.2 in.) |
| Curb weight | 2180 kg (4805 lb.) |
| Fuel consumption | 14.7 ltr/100 km (16 mpg) |

The new Lincoln Aviator has come out of the same mold that produced the Navigator last year, although it is slightly smaller. Such is the consistency of the design, this new model is quite simply a midsized replica of its rather gross brother. With the Navigator, Lincoln already holds a leading 40% share of the premium SUV market, so it hopes that adding this new mainstream version will inflate its market share significantly.

The chromed signature waterfall grille, with its dark vanes, and large, clear-lens headlights dominate the Aviator's "face." The lower bumper adds to its aggressive stance, with body-colored cladding wrapping around the wheel arches and lower sections of all four doors to protect against chips, dents, and door dings. Full-length running boards are integrated into the sill but are not powered like the Navigator's. Chrome is carefully used to pick out the grille surround, waistline, roof rack, and rear number-plate surround.

Inside, the design direction is also taken from the Navigator, with the same blend of Lincoln design cues—satin nickel, American walnut-burr wood, leather, and more than a hundred white light-emitting diodes (LED) that illuminate the instruments and most buttons and controls, and complement the satin-nickel finish. The prominence of the analog clock is now becoming a traditional touch across all Lincoln-brand cars. A band of wood works its way around the cabin, providing a visual waistline to draw the eye to its extremities and making it seem more spacious.

The "Russian doll" approach has worked for other manufacturers, notably BMW with its 3, 5, and 7 Series family. And it should prove a lucrative strategy for Lincoln.

# Lincoln Navicross

| Design | Gerry McGovern |
|---|---|
| Engine | 4.2 V8 |
| Gearbox | 5-speed automatic |
| Installation | Front-engined/all-wheel drive |
| Brakes front/rear | Discs/discs, EBD, HDC (Hill Descent Control) |
| Front tires | 255/50/R20 |
| Rear tires | 255/50/R20 |
| Length | 4741 mm (187 in.) |
| Width | 1862 mm (73.3 in.) |
| Height | 1500 mm (59.1 in.) |
| Wheelbase | 2900 mm (114.2 in.) |
| Track front/rear | 1634/1652 mm (64.3/65 in.) |

The Navicross is the most recent in a line of concept cars by Gerry McGovern and represents the latest step in the creation of Lincoln's new design DNA.

Based on a modified Lincoln LS platform, it uses a combination of coupé proportions with the swept screen, short trunk lid, and other characteristics of an SUV. But the Navicross is actually a four-door car, with door handles well hidden in its lavish chrome trim. It has no B-pillars, so the rear doors are rear-hinged, giving easier access to the seats; this was an iconic feature of the classic 1962 "clap-door" Lincoln Continental.

Inside, the Navicross is inviting and indulgent. The encased seats are trimmed with aniline leather, and hair-on-hide is used on the door trim panels. Important to Lincoln's heritage is the symmetrical instrument panel, which holds voice-activated LED viewing screens and has evolved from that first seen on the Continental concept in 2002.

The wheels look oversized for the body; or, at least, such an elegant car might look better if it sat closer to the ground, but could gain extra ground clearance by using an air-suspension system when needed off-road. However, this is intentional. Lincoln is testing reaction to a new car with dramatic proportions, one with elegant surfaces and chrome strips, that could go off-road without relying on the usual lower-body protection seen on such vehicles. The question is, would anyone want to use the Navicross like an SUV, and actually get it dirty?

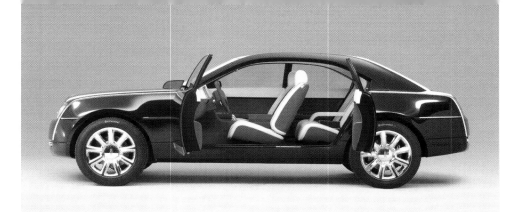

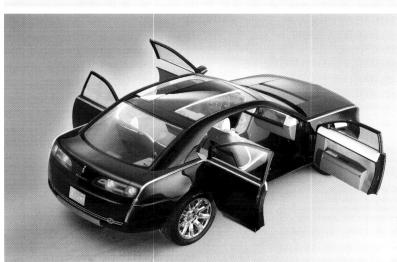

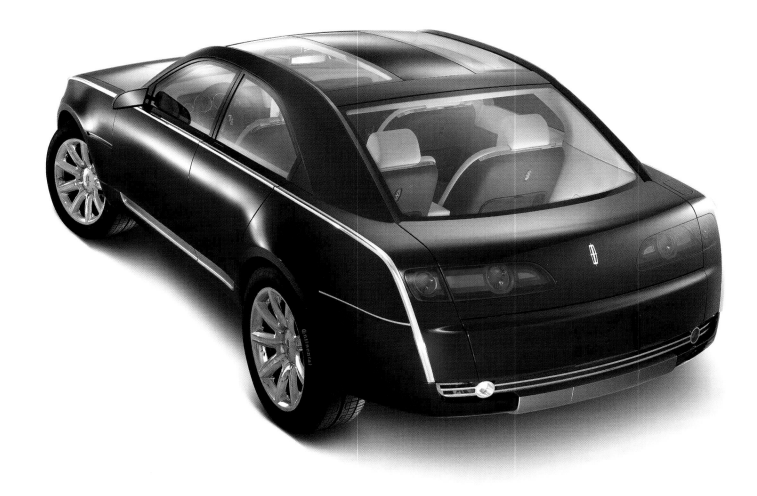

# Matra P75

| Design | Vincent Olivier |
|---|---|
| Engine | Induction motor |
| Power | 50 kW (67 bhp) @ 4000–10,000 rpm |
| Front tires | 195/65/R15 |
| Rear tires | 195/65/R15 |
| Length | 3540 mm (139.4 in.) |
| Width | 1730 mm (68.1 in.) |
| Height | 1750 mm (68.9 in.) |
| Curb weight | 1080 kg (2381 lb.) |
| 0–100 km/h (62 mph) | 14.5 sec |
| Top speed | 140 km/h (87 mph) |

For many years, Matra has worked closely with its compatriot Renault, designing and building the original Espace, and latterly they built the Avantime together. At one time, Matra made its own models, too, a long-running series of sports cars, including the Bagheera and Murena, and now it has developed a new one: the tiny M72 fun car.

But this is the first time Matra has crossed the Atlantic with its own new concept, the P75, and shown it to the motor industry giants in the USA. It's a modular urban transport concept, a compact four-seater MPV that was part of the Michelin Design Challenge, dedicated in 2002 to French design.

The P75 is essentially a bold, French-designed mono-volume with a steeply raked front screen and a high-level roof, which together give it a spacious interior. Innovative systems include twin rear doors that slide open sideways from the center. Matra is expert at composite technology and has used this in the construction of the P75. The chassis is made from a sandwich of composite and stainless steel, while the exterior is plastic composite.

Because the occupants sit higher than in a normal car, space is available under the floor to take various power sources, including a gasoline or natural gas tank, or even batteries.

Inside, the design offers a light and airy space, with large side windows and windshield providing aexcellent visibility—ideal for city driving. Relaxing colors are used for the seats and instrument panel, which has a screen incorporating the dials and the navigation system.

It can only be a positive thing for Matra to be in Detroit with its P75, touting for business, but you can't help thinking that if the P75 were a new V8-powered, Espace-sized MPV it might better capture the hearts and minds of America's heads of industry. And the closure of Matra's main plant, after the Avantime was axed early in 2003, probably means that this is the last design from the idiosyncratic French company.

# Maybach

| Design | Professor Gaus and Stephen Mattin |
|---|---|
| Engine | 5.5 V12 |
| Power | 405 kW (543 bhp) @ 5250 rpm |
| Torque | 900 Nm (663 lb. ft) @ 2300–3000 rpm |
| Gearbox | 5-speed automatic |
| Installation | Front-engined/rear-wheel drive |
| Front suspension | Double wishbone |
| Rear suspension | Multi-link |
| Brakes front/rear | Discs/discs, SBC, ABS, BA, ESP |
| Front tires | 275/50R19 |
| Rear tires | 275/50R19 |
| Length | 6165 mm (242.7 in.) |
| Width | 1980 mm (78 in.) |
| Height | 1573 mm (61.9 in.) |
| Wheelbase | 3827 mm (150.7 in.) |
| Track front/rear | 1675/1695 mm (65.9/66.7 in.) |
| Curb weight | 2855 kg (6294 lb.) |
| 0–100 km/h (62 mph) | 5.4 sec |
| Top speed | 250 km/h (155 mph) |
| Fuel consumption | 15.9 ltr/100 km (14.8 mpg) |

"Massive" and "stately" are probably the best words to describe the DaimlerChrysler group's new Maybach. Previewed in our last edition as an almost-gelled concept, here is the plutocrat-ready 62 in all the patrician glory of its 6.2-meter (20.3 ft) length. And if you don't need limousine proportions, or can't quite afford the 62, then there is the Maybach 57 to consider: 5.7 meters (18.6 ft) is still impressive.

The style is grand yet restful and, prospective owners may be pleased to know, should stand the test of time. A gently curving chrome arc runs the entire length of the Maybach, delineating the two-tone colors and accenting its fairly elegant side profile. Still, the Maybach is nothing like as ostentatious as, say, a Bentley Arnage or Continental, or any Rolls-Royce. As a much more exclusive alternative to the Mercedes S-Class, it is a car more likely to be occupied by heads of state than lottery winners.

The Maybach is no slouch. It has more power and torque than any other series-produced sedan on the planet, with a 406-kW (543-bhp), twin-turbocharged V12 engine that will thunder it to 100 km/h (62 mph) in just 5.4 seconds, a figure more often associated with brands like Porsche, and remarkable for a car of its weight.

Status is guaranteed with Maybach ownership, but the real benefit to hard-working politicians or business leaders comes in being chauffeured in such opulence. An inviting mix of warm leather and crafted wood draws you into the spacious interior, a place where comfort and technology go hand in hand. In the rear of the Maybach 62 the seats recline and foot supports extend, offering a sit-back-and-relax position at the push of a button. A 600-watt stereo system, a DVD player, telephones, a fridge, and a TV make the experience of both the Maybach 62 and the 57 more akin to traveling by luxury private jet.

# Mazda2

| | |
|---|---|
| Design | Moray Callum |
| Engine | 1.6 in-line 4 (1.25 and 1.4 in-line 4, and 1.6 in-line 4 diesel, also offered) |
| Power | 75 kW (100 bhp) |
| Torque | 146 Nm (108 lb. ft) @ 4000 rpm |
| Gearbox | 5-speed manual |
| Installation | Front-engined/front-wheel drive |
| Front suspension | MacPherson strut |
| Rear suspension | Torsion beam |
| Brakes front/rear | Discs/drums |
| Length | 3925 mm (154.5 in.) |
| Width | 1680 mm (66.1 in.) |
| Height | 1545 mm (60.9 in.) |
| Wheelbase | 2490 mm (98 in.) |
| Track front/rear | 1470/1445 mm (57.9/56.9 in.) |
| 0–100 km/h (62 mph) | 11.4 sec |
| Top speed | 180 km/h (112 mph) |
| Fuel consumption | 7.1 ltr/100 km (33.1 mpg) |
| $CO_2$ emissions | 168 g/km |

The real-time version of the MX Sport Runabout concept shown at Geneva in 2002, the new Mazda2 aims to follow the new brand DNA of this manufacturer by being "stylish, insightful, and spirited" at the same time as satisfying market demand in both Japan and Europe.

But this doesn't really tell the whole story, for in reality the Mazda2 is based wholesale on the platform of the recently launched Ford Fiesta. And, with its relatively conservative design approach, this little Ford has not caused many waves.

Consequently, the Mazda2—despite rather more pronounced design flourishes—also appears to struggle to find a unique styling direction. The grille is distinctively Mazda, there are sporting lines, and, all in all, nothing really offends, but it feels as if Mazda needs to reconsider its style direction, as Nissan has done, rather than seeking to emulate a mix of Alfa Romeo and Seat. This is an extremely competitive sector, where high sales volumes are essential to recover large development costs. The exterior lacks excitement, and that might hamper sales if Mazda has ambitions to court younger buyers.

The dark, sporty interior makes extensive use of aluminum on the center console. It works better than the exterior, probably because it was designed at Mazda's European studio, whereas the exterior was finished in Japan.

Maybe the Mazda2 will be a big hit in Japan, but it really is doubtful that it has what it takes to become a top seller in Europe. That brand DNA has a rogue gene in there somewhere.

# Mazda MX Sportif

| Design | Moray Callum |
|---|---|
| Engine | 2.0 in-line 4 |
| Power | 110 kW (148 bhp) @ 6000 rpm |
| Torque | 187 Nm (138 lb. ft) @ 4500 rpm |
| Gearbox | 5-speed manual |
| Installation | Front-engined/front-wheel drive |
| Front suspension | MacPherson strut |
| Rear suspension | Multi-link |
| Brakes front/rear | Discs/discs |
| Front tires | 225/45R18 |
| Rear tires | 225/45R18 |
| Length | 4350 mm (171.3 in.) |
| Width | 1760 mm (69.3 in.) |
| Height | 1450 mm (57.1 in.) |
| Wheelbase | 2640 mm (104 in.) |
| Track front/rear | 1535/1530 mm (60.4/60.2 in.) |

Mazda unveiled the MX Sportif at the 2003 Geneva International Motor Show. This new design concept, once again, is supposed to dovetail neatly with Mazda's core product DNA, which is defined by distinctive design, exceptional functionality, and responsive performance and handling.

The design begins with the dynamic proportions and taut contours of the long cabin and is accentuated by the extremely short overhangs. Sturdy lines extend from the prominent grille and reach back through the hood to combine with triangular rear pillars, producing a powerful, confident form. The Sportif's well-planted stance is enhanced by the roofline and aggressively flared wings, while its strong shoulders give it dynamism.

The front view highlights the relatively upright sides, and their minimal tumble angle—the inward slope of the side windows—increases headroom for the occupants. The unique resin grille, inset door handles, and shapely tailgate also add to the MX Sportif's distinctive persona.

Inside, Mazda presents a sporty design with an overall ambience that evokes visual excitement. Materials have been carefully selected for their texture and appearance. The instrument panel and door trim have simple, clean-cut forms that add to the sense of openness and spaciousness. Finished in a high-gloss piano black, the center console assures good visibility for the driver. Its illumination is the blackout type, but, when the lights are switched on, amber-red backlighting is augmented by indirect blue lighting to create a pleasant glow. This is intended to alleviate eyestrain.

# Mazda Washu

| | |
|---|---|
| Design | Moray Callum |
| Engine | 3.5 V6 |
| Power | 180 kW (241 bhp) @ 6500 rpm |
| Torque | 278 Nm (205 lb. ft) @ 3500 rpm |
| Gearbox | 6-speed automatic |
| Front suspension | Double wishbone |
| Rear suspension | Multi-link |
| Brakes front/rear | Discs/discs |
| Front tires | 225-750R540A PAX |
| Rear tires | 225-750R540A PAX |
| Length | 4830 mm (190.2 in.) |
| Width | 1850 mm (72.8 in.) |
| Height | 1570 mm (61.8 in.) |
| Wheelbase | 3200 mm (126 in.) |
| Track front/rear | 1560/1600 mm (61.4/63 in.) |

The Washu is the first of a new series of concept and production cars that Mazda will unveil in 2003 under the design direction of Moray Callum.

A car with solid proportions and modern surfaces, it sits glued to the ground, thanks to its low body and tire-hugging wheel arches. Washu means "eagle's wing" in Japanese, and Mazda claims that this idea is reflected in the appearance of the doors, saying that these, when fully open, make the car look just like an eagle with outstretched wings.

The clean front wraps around to the LED headlights, complete with an auto-focusing system, and then over the "clam shell" hood to the pronounced wheel arches. Note the absence of door mirrors, to maintain a clutter-free look. The windshield glass splits at the front header, and new glass roof panels begin running either side of a central structure that extends along the roof's entire length. The B-pillars sit inboard of the doors to give the illusion of a structural hoop halfway along the car.

Inside, the space is flexible, with a strong architectural quality. Captain's chairs and steer-by-wire technology allow the driver—in theory, at least, on this show car—to store the steering wheel inside the instrument panel when the car is parked; an ID card then deploys the instrument panel and steering wheel into the driving position.

The interior design has a sound sense of structure, with sculpted surfaces and a combination of technical colors to create a functional, if austere, ambience.

# MCC Smart Roadster/ Roadster-Coupé

| | |
|---|---|
| Engine | 0.7 in-line 3 roadster-coupé |
| Power | 60 kW (80 bhp) @ 5250 rpm |
| Torque | 110 Nm (81 lb. ft) @ 3000 rpm |
| Gearbox | 6-speed sequential automated |
| Installation | Rear-engined/rear-wheel drive |
| Front suspension | MacPherson strut |
| Rear suspension | De Dion with wishbone |
| Brakes front/rear | Discs/drums, ESP |
| Front tires | 205/50R15 |
| Rear tires | 205/50R15 |
| Length | 3427 mm (134.9 in.) |
| Width | 1615 mm (63.6 in.) |
| Height | 1192 mm (46.9 in.) |
| Wheelbase | 2360 mm (92.9 in.) |
| Track front/rear | 1357/1392 mm (53.4/54.8 in.) |
| 0–100 km/h (62 mph) | 11.2 sec |
| Top speed | 175 km/h (109 mph) |
| Fuel consumption | 5.5 ltr/100 km (42.8 mpg) |

The original Smart City Coupé has become ubiquitous in Europe's capital cities, but it is almost four years since the brand was officially created, and only now has the DaimlerChrysler-owned MCC company launched a major new product: the Smart Roadster. And, in its way, it is as offbeat as the stubby original.

Two versions, a convertible and a coupé, arrive in showrooms in 2003. Mazda has ruled the small sports-car arena for years with its MX-5, with some competition from the MGF and Fiat Barchetta. But the Smart Roadster is smaller than them all, more akin to the iconic 1991 Honda Beat and—for those with longer motoring memories—the 1958 Austin-Healey "Frogeye" Sprite. Tiny, though, they are not: one sacrifice Smart devotees must make is the 2.5-meter (8.2 ft) length, which made end-on parking possible with the City Coupé, and so was a key selling point in ever-more crowded urban Europe. At 3.4 meters (11.2 ft) long, the Roadster is a juggernaut by comparison.

Nevertheless, unmistakable design and cool branding are destined to propel it up the sales charts. Smart design principles have been faithfully adhered to. As on the City Coupé, the Tridion safety cell encircles the body below and behind the doors, and the windshield is color-matched to provide the Smart Roadster's two-tone uniqueness.

The design of Smart cars has defied surface conventions. Their exteriors are broken up not only by different colors but also by different textures and materials. Therefore, the design of a Smart is perceived differently by the onlooker: tight panel gaps, for instance, are less critical, as the eye is drawn to the overall design rather than such details. "Product design" is an alternative description. The result is extremely effective and projects an ample sense of fun and excitement.

The engine is still rear-mounted, with a low driving position similar to that of a Lotus Elise, and the car is set close to the road for good handling. The interior is simple and contemporary, with snug-fitting seats.

It is hard to see how this new Smart can fail to win the hearts of its buyers.

# Mercury Messenger

| Design | Gerry McGovern |
|---|---|
| Engine | 4.6 V8 |
| Gearbox | 6-speed automatic |
| Installation | Front-engined/rear-wheel drive |
| Brakes front/rear | Discs/discs, EBD |
| Front tires | 275/40/R19 |
| Rear tires | 305/40R20 |
| Length | 4533 mm (178.5 in.) |
| Width | 1938 mm (76.3 in.) |
| Height | 1304 mm (51.3 in.) |
| Wheelbase | 2825 mm (111.2 in.) |
| Track front/rear | 1662/1650 mm (65.4/65 in.) |

Mercury, Ford's US-only upmarket brand, will introduce four new products over the next four years, including a minivan, a small SUV, and two conventional cars. The Messenger coupé concept gives a strong hint of the design that will lead this rather undistinguished make's rejuvenation.

As the messenger of the heavens, the god Mercury was associated with speed and agility in ancient Roman mythology. So the new Messenger concept was fittingly chosen to be a dynamic two-seater coupé, driver-focused, and made from aluminum for lightness, and, therefore, nimble dynamics.

The long hood leads to a "fast" windshield, then to a roof that quickly falls away before descending to the short trunk lid—a silhouette very like the BMW Z8's, familiar to millions of James Bond fans. The sense of speed is helped by the reclining door glass and the door opening line that leads up to the top of the rear windshield. At the front, the headlights appear to be stacked above the air intakes set into the bumper. This idea is also reflected at the back, where the rear lights stack above the exhaust tailpipes.

The strong sculpted feature running through the doors and the air-scoops in the hood indicates the V8 power lurking beneath. The wheels use a turbine theme for their spokes: the Mercury "flying M" logo. The interior is modern and functional, with minimal instrumentation; the door-panel design echoes the shape of the exterior body side and emphasizes the perception of a protective environment.

This is a well-executed design, which is just what Mercury needs if it's going to compete properly against GM's sporty brands.

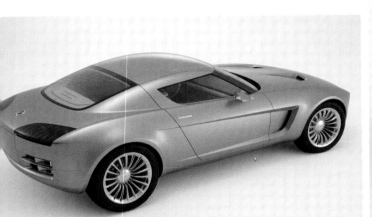

# Mercury Monterey

The new Mercury Monterey is practically the same car as the Ford Freestar minivan. The two models share identical dimensions and packaging for the 4.2 V6 powertrain. They also share most of their components, with only subtle visible differences, although the Monterey is positioned slightly higher in the market than the Freestar. The Monterey targets buyers in their thirties to mid-forties who want the functionality of a minivan allied to a luxurious interior.

The most visible differences between the two cars are the Monterey's "waterfall" grille, the satin bezel of the tail lights and fog lights, and aluminum finishes on the handles of the doors and the tailgate, and on the roof rack. Machined wheels complete the look and mirror the satin aluminum accents.

Mercury claims that, from now on, all its new cars will be clean and simple, with lean and taut surface language. This sounds like Ford's own design language, so the implication is that Mercury must subsist by using Ford's extensive parts bin but with limited individuality. Denigrate this strategy if you will, but it has served Ford well since Edsel Ford invented the Mercury make in 1938; it was an early example of platform sharing and has meant Ford can wring even more sales out of individual designs.

One special luxury feature of the Monterey is the heated and cooled front seats. These were first introduced on the Lincoln Navigator, and function by heated or cooled air being directed through the seat backs and cushions.

The Monterey is launched in 2003 to complement the updated 2003 Grand Marquis, the all-new 2003 Marauder, and the Mercury Mountaineer. The US minivan market accounts for more than one million sales each year, and further growth is expected at the luxury $30,000-plus price level. Ford must hope its Mercury brand will be able, with the help of a variety of marketing initiatives, to gather more sales for the company than the Ford Freestar alone could bring in.

| | |
|---|---|
| Design | Darrell Behmer |
| Engine | 4.2 V6 |
| Power | 150 kW (201 bhp) @ 4250 rpm |
| Torque | 360 Nm (265 lb. ft) @ 3500 rpm |
| Gearbox | 4-speed automatic |
| Installation | Front-engined/front-wheel drive |
| Front suspension | MacPherson strut |
| Rear suspension | Twist beam |
| Brakes front/rear | Discs/discs, ABS, EBD |
| Front tires | P235/60R16 |
| Rear tires | P235/60R16 |
| Length | 5105 mm (201 in.) |
| Width | 1946 mm (76.6 in.) |
| Height | 1745 mm (68.7 in.) |
| Wheelbase | 3068 mm (120.8 in.) |
| Track front/rear | 1633/1600 mm (64.3/63 in.) |
| Kerb weight | 1999 kg (4406 lb.) |

# MG XPower SV

The new XPower SV is a dramatic reinterpretation of a prestigious MG sports car—very different from the X80 concept first shown at the Frankfurt Motor Show in 2001. The new car is still based on a Qvale chassis but is no longer a grand tourer: this is a high-performance coupé aimed much more squarely at the driving enthusiast, and with aggressive styling to match.

At the extreme end of the market, a massively powerful 720-kW (965-bhp) version is planned for track use only, and all roadgoing models of the car will be marketed under the MG Sport & Racing XPower brand.

The exterior styling owes much to the demands of airflow management, with slatted front wings and a large spoiler at the rear. Exterior panels are all made from carbon fiber to minimize weight, while front and rear diffusers are fitted underneath to manage the airflow for high-speed stability.

Inside, the SV is like a racing car, with Sparco carbon-shell racing seats, a spare wheel in the cabin, custom helmet-storage areas, four-point electrically locking harnesses, and Motec racing instruments.

The styling is certainly a bit "boy racer," but if the new SV performs as its pulse-raising specification promises, and the customer versions (which will probably be built in Italy) possess decent build quality, hard-core enthusiasts with plenty of disposable income will probably be ready to pay the necessary price. MG can then offer an impressive new "halo" product. But other new MG products must follow on quickly to capitalize on the media attention the new SV will surely generate.

| Design | Peter Stevens |
|---|---|
| Engine | 5.0 V8 |
| 0–100 km/h (62 mph) | 4.4 sec |
| Top speed | 314 km/h (195 mph) limited |

# Mitsubishi Endeavor

| Engine | 3.8 V6 |
|---|---|
| Power | 160 kW (215 bhp) @ 5000 rpm |
| Torque | 339 Nm (250 lb. ft) @ 3750 rpm |
| Gearbox | 4-speed automatic |
| Installation | Front-engined/all-wheel drive |
| Front suspension | MacPherson strut |
| Rear suspension | Multi-link |
| Brakes front/rear | Discs/discs |
| Front tires | 235/65R17 |
| Rear tires | 235/65R17 |
| Length | 4830 mm (190.2 in.) |
| Width | 1870 mm (73.6 in.) |
| Height | 1710 mm (67.3 in.) |
| Wheelbase | 2750 mm (108.3 in.) |
| Track front/rear | 1600/1600 mm (63/63 in.) |
| Curb weight | 1885 kg (4156 lb.) |

The production version of the new Mitsubishi Endeavor was designed at Mitsubishi Motors' Design Center in Cypress, California, and engineered at its research and development site in Ann Arbor, Michigan. It will compete in the midsized SUV market against cars such as the Toyota Highlander, the Honda Pilot, and Nissan's new Murano.

The Endeavor's strong, two-box shape has several dominant features. At the front the large hood conceals the V6 engine, while the angular headlight clusters flank the dual slatted grilles. These are just above a strong lower bumper that incorporates opposing fog lights, separated by a gaping lower air vent.

Large wheel arches come complete with ample wheel clearance and appear chiseled rather than molded into shape, wrapping around the wheels aggressively. A forceful feature line runs the length of the side between them. Roof bars sit aloft the flat roof, which leads to the slightly inclined tailgate and compact rear lights.

The stylish and sporty interior has distinctive dashboard and instrument panel lighting that makes extensive use of blue LEDs. The Endeavor shares some interior styling cues with the Eclipse, notably the soft-touch dashboard surfaces. Just behind the leather steering wheel, Mitsubishi has integrated a trio of well-designed, aluminum-accented instrument dials, industrially large for effective readouts.

The Endeavor is available in front-wheel-drive and all-wheel-drive versions, and arrived in showrooms in March 2003 as a 2004 model.

# Mitsubishi Tarmac Spyder

| Engine | 2.0 in-line 4 |
|---|---|
| Power | 224 kW (300 bhp) |
| Gearbox | 5-speed automatic |
| Installation | Front-engined/all-wheel drive |
| Front tires | 225/35R19 |
| Rear tires | 225/35R19 |
| Length | 4055 mm (159.7 in.) |
| Width | 1825 mm (71.9 in.) |
| Wheelbase | 2515 mm (99 in.) |

Youthful and extreme, the Tarmac Spyder concept is a two-plus-two aimed at the techno-savvy young Generation Y market, and is a follow-up to the CZ-3 Tarmac sports hatchback shown in 2001. Supposed to be fun to drive, the car has racy lines; proportionally, it's a dramatic wedge that begins at the front grille and rises sharply up to the waistline and on to the trunk lid.

At the front, there is a stark contrast between the narrow "arrowhead" headlights alongside the hood and the wide-open "mouth" that is built into the front bumper. This mouth makes the car look aggressive and manly, but it's very necessary for the massive cooling needed by the engine. The door mirrors echo the car's overall spearhead shape.

The Spyder comes with a detachable top, which lets Mitsubishi offer rear seats as standard. More acceptable today is to have a folding roof and a retractable top, and make the car a dedicated two-seater. The Ford Streetka (see p. 110), although only offered as a traditional soft-top, would be a competitor if the Spyder were ever produced, because it's a great example of a dedicated two-seater package.

The dashboard and instrument panel use wave-line styling themes. A camera mounted in the door mirrors can record a journey or play it on individual LED monitors to the front and rear passengers. The interior scheme is racing-car-inspired, with body-hugging seats and a highly functional aura.

# Nissan Evalia

| Design | Christopher Reitz |
| --- | --- |
| Engine | 2.5 in-line 4 |
| Power | 121 kW (162 bhp) @ 6000 rpm |
| Torque | 230 Nm (169 lb. ft) @ 3000 rpm |
| Gearbox | 7-speed CVT |
| Installation | Front-engined/front-wheel drive |
| Front tires | 19 in. PAX |
| Rear tires | 19 in. PAX |
| Length | 4300 mm (169.3 in.) |
| Height | 1510 mm (59.4 in.) |
| Wheelbase | 2700 mm (106.3 in.) |

The Evalia is one of those innovative concept cars that really do bring fresh ideas to the automotive world. Designed at Nissan's newly opened studio in Paddington, London, it is intended to replace the decidedly lackluster Almera Tino C-segment mini-MPV.

As a compact family car, the Evalia cunningly adds coupé design lines to a hatchback body style. Nissan is aiming here for a practical car for families but at the same time one that gives the weary father the spirit-lifting feel of a sports model. Does this compromise comfort? Not too much, because Nissan only provides the thrills with a sporty seating position and taut sports suspension—nothing extreme.

The Evalia concept features double-hinged barn-type doors with no B-pillars. This means that, were this a real-life car, the sills and roof would need to be substantially stronger than those of a normal sedan to meet current side-impact safety standards, let alone future ones.

At the front, Nissan's "flying wings" theme is prominent, with the split insets at the front of the hood reaching out above and below the headlights. The front and rear lights follow the vertical design of the Nissan 350Z sports car, while at the rear the tailgate extends deep into the roof with a wide, wrap-around rear window and a surf-tail roofline above.

Inside, there is more innovation: four "floating" seats are supported on a central rail that has an integrated child seat that doubles as a baby buggy when locked on to a separate three-wheeled frame. The dashboard, which takes its inspiration from a biplane wing, conceals a combined fridge-microwave unit. Diffused lighting in white or orange can be selected to suit the driver's mood and there is a neat touch in the trunk: ninety-nine embedded "trackballs" make loading easier and electrically retract once the luggage is rolled in.

This is a well-executed concept, and if it became the next Tino while retaining its appealing design flourishes it would sell well.

# Nissan Maxima

| | |
|---|---|
| Engine | 3.5 V6 |
| Power | 194 kW (260 bhp) |
| Torque | 339 Nm (250 lb. ft) |
| Gearbox | 5-speed automatic with clutchless manual facility |
| Installation | Front-engined/front-wheel drive |
| Front suspension | MacPherson strut |
| Rear suspension | Multi-link |
| Brakes front/rear | Discs/discs, EBD, BA |
| Front tires | P245/45R18 |
| Rear tires | P245/45R18 |
| Length | 4915 mm (193.5 in.) |
| Width | 1821 mm (71.7 in.) |
| Height | 1481 mm (58.3 in.) |
| Wheelbase | 2824 mm (111.2 in.) |
| Track front/rear | 1549/1554 mm (61/61.2 in.) |
| Curb weight | 1557 kg (3432 lb.) |
| Fuel consumption | 8.1 ltr/100 km (29 mpg) |

The Maxima is now in its sixth generation, and Nissan claims the car has an extremely loyal customer base, with many buyers on their fourth or fifth. In this desirable situation, the dilemma for designers is that they must continually evolve and improve the product without changing it so much that they frighten away their existing customers.

For the new Maxima, Nissan's designers aimed to create an exterior design that captures the characteristics of a performance car and a luxury sedan. They did this by combining the gentle lines and unemotional surfaces of the lower body with sculpted wheel arches and an upper body possessing much sportier elements, such as a rising waistline, an arched coupé-like roof, and a short trunk lid complete with lip spoiler. The roof arch continues to the trunk lid, so the single arc is retained when the car is seen from the side, but the rear windshield drops at a steeper angle to ensure that the trunk opening is adequate.

The front end is clean, with large areas of body-colored surface, large, decidedly Nissan headlights, and the distinctive Nissan signature grille with its chrome finish.

Inside, the Maxima's Skyview roof, a single, elongated, rectangular glass panel, creates an open environment for every passenger. Black leather and aluminum trim meets gray switchgear in a modern, sporty, if unremarkable, interior.

Motoring pundits have generally found previous Maximas wanting in both design charisma and driving appeal. Despite Nissan's pronouncements about loyalty, the Maxima has been, until now, at best second-rate. Then again, there is no doubting its traditional Nissan quality and reliability. So it's very likely that this is another totally safe bet for aficionados.

# Nissan Micra

| | |
|---|---|
| Design | Christopher Reitz |
| Engine | 1.4 in-line 4 (1.0 and 1.2 in-line 4, and 1.5 in-line 4 turbo-diesel, also offered) |
| Power | 65 kW (88 bhp) @ 5600 rpm |
| Torque | 128 Nm (94 lb. ft) @ 3200 rpm |
| Gearbox | 5-speed manual |
| Installation | Front-engined/front-wheel drive |
| Front suspension | MacPherson strut |
| Rear suspension | Torsion beam |
| Brakes front/rear | Discs/drums, ABS, EBD, BA |
| Front tires | 175/60R15 |
| Rear tires | 175/60R15 |
| Length | 3715 mm (146.3 in.) |
| Width | 1660 mm (65.4 in.) |
| Height | 1525 mm (60 in.) |
| Wheelbase | 2430 mm (95.7 in.) |
| Track front/rear | 1470/1445 mm (57.9/56.9 in.) |
| Fuel consumption | 6.3 ltr/100 km (37.3 mpg) |

The old Nissan Micra has had a loyal following since its launch in 1993, when it even won the European Car of the Year award. These days, however, the Nissan–Renault business alliance is at full steam, and the fruits of the partnership are being realized.

As a result the new Micra has a much stronger visual identity, a trait Renault has been anxious to instill in Nissan's previously rather mundane fare (although the old Micra was one of the more pleasing examples of design under the former all-Japanese regime). The first new Nissan to benefit from the skills of Patrick le Quément, Renault's design king, was the new Primera.

Nissan believes the new car will appeal to a younger market than the old model, a sound strategy for getting more people hooked on Nissans at an early age. Chic, confident yet friendly styling is the theme, with strong, sculpted surfaces and striking features.

The rounded upper architecture sits above the body, which has a bold step that runs the length of the car. The headlights are mounted higher, which allows the grille to extend outboard to mask the indicators, and make the car look wider and more stable.

The cabin is trimmed in two-tone gray, plain and contemporary, with ivory-colored instrument switches and a natty three-spoke steering wheel.

Also shown at the Paris Motor Show in 2002 was the Micra C+C concept, a convertible version with folding top. This is expected to reach production in 2005, and when it does it will provide stiff competition for the Peugeot 206CC—particularly if it has Nissan's legendary quality, an area where the Italian-made 206CC has been weak—and will further increase the youthful appeal of the model.

# Nissan Murano

| Design | Nissan's studio in Japan |
|---|---|
| Engine | 3.5 V6 |
| Power | 179 kW (240 bhp) |
| Gearbox | Automatic CVT |
| Installation | Front-engined/all-wheel drive |
| Front suspension | MacPherson strut |
| Rear suspension | Multi-link |
| Brakes front/rear | Discs/discs, BA, EBD |
| Front tires | R18 |
| Rear tires | R18 |
| Length | 4765 mm (187.6 in.) |
| Width | 1880 mm (74 in.) |
| Height | 1689 mm (66.5 in.) |
| Wheelbase | 2850 mm (111.2 in.) |

Nissan's success in the SUV market with the original Pathfinder and the Xterra seems set to continue with the new Murano, a crossover SUV designed specifically for the North American market. But where Nissans have tended to trail the pack gingerly in terms of visual innovation, the Murano leaps well ahead with its modern aesthetic, to compete head-on with the influential new Chrysler Pacifica.

The name derives from an island near Venice, in Italy, renowned for its sculpted glass. The artisans of Murano are considered leaders in both cutting-edge design and glassmaking technology. The car's exterior design links Nissan brand values neatly with these qualities. Its sporty presence is built around a rising waistline, which culminates in the triangulated D-pillar that wraps over the rear lights and tailgate.

A similarly sporty look for the interior is achieved through the combination of sculpted interior surfaces on the instrument panel and seats with aluminum detailing throughout. The whole impression is of a solidity that is easy on the eye, with controls that are easy to find.

The seats are set in a commanding position and enough ground clearance is provided for fairly energetic off-road pursuits. Nissan's continuously variable transmission (CVT) eliminates the "steps" between gears, ensuring a smoother operation by keeping the engine in its optimum power range whatever driving and load conditions arise. This system is especially useful in long, uphill drives, eliminating the customary hunt for the proper gear.

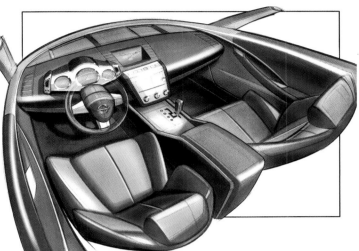

# Nissan Quest

| Engine | 3.5 V6 |
|---|---|
| Power | 172 kW (230 bhp) |
| Torque | 319 Nm (235 lb. ft) |
| Gearbox | 5-speed automatic |
| Installation | Front-engined/front-wheel drive |
| Front suspension | MacPherson strut |
| Rear suspension | Multi-link |
| Brakes front/rear | Discs/discs, ABS, BA, EBD |
| Front tires | 225/60R17 |
| Rear tires | 225/60R17 |
| Length | 5184 mm (204.1 in.) |
| Width | 1971 mm (77.6 in.) |
| Height | 1778 mm (70 in.) |
| Wheelbase | 3150 mm (124 in.) |
| Track front/rear | 1699/1699 mm (66.9/66.9 in.) |

Trying to create an object of desire when designing a minivan is one of the trickiest tasks in car design today. Compromise on functionality, and your car will be massively criticized, because function is deemed to be a minivan's prime purpose. For this reason the results are often unprepossessing boxes on wheels that stimulate precious little emotion in onlookers or, crucially, potential owners. To put it bluntly, most MPVs are boring.

For the Quest, Nissan's designers have really tried to get round this problem, and have gone for a one-and-a-half-box shape that stretches out to a length of 5.2 meters (17.9 ft) but retains curvaceous design cues in its roofline and in the waistline, which is initiated by the headlights and then weaves its way backward, visually separating the forward cabin from the rear passenger space.

At the front, the grille and headlights are unmistakably the new face of Nissan, while the rear lights sit outside the tailgate, emphasizing the car's width.

Although sliding rear doors must be upright enough to allow the door and its mechanism to slide outside the fixed body, the Quest's design manages to include some curved form in them and gives the wheel arches some flair, to project a certain sportiness.

The contemporary interior is noteworthy: the Skyview roof has four panoramic glass windows and a rear, overhead, aircraft-style console with personal reading lights and air vents, as well as twin DVD display screens. Other innovations include a low-height instrument panel, set in the center of the dashboard, that also contains the gearshift and myriad storage compartments.

This is a sterling effort at putting some visual interest into an everyday car without chipping away at its practicality.

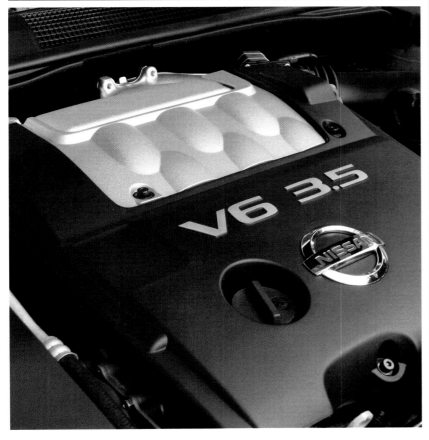

# Nissan Titan

| | |
|---|---|
| Engine | 5.6 V8 |
| Power | 224 kW (300 bhp) |
| Torque | 509 Nm (375 lb. ft) |
| Gearbox | 5-speed automatic |
| Installation | Front-engined/4-wheel drive |
| Front suspension | Double wishbone |
| Rear suspension | Leaf spring |
| Brakes front/rear | Discs/discs, ABS |
| Front tyres | 265/70R18 |
| Rear tyres | 265/70R18 |
| Length | 5695 mm (224.2 in.) |
| Width | 2002 mm (78.8 in.) |
| Height | 1890 mm (74.4 in.) |
| Wheelbase | 3550 mm (139.8 in.) |
| Track front/rear | 1715/1715 mm (67.5/67.5 in.) |

Titan is Nissan's first-ever model in the full-sized truck category, and will be offered late in 2003 as both King Cab and Crew Cab derivatives.

The Titan name was chosen to reflect the marketing importance Nissan places on the truck's size and power. The company's own research has concluded that the key elements in the successful design of a full-sized pickup continue to be horsepower, torque, towing capacity, a large cab, and an enormous load bed.

Designed at Nissan's studio in California, the Titan has a distinctive front end with large proportions. One detail that differentiates it from other models is the expanse of chrome on the grille and bumper. The hood, which has a large, raised center section designed to clear the engine, is quite flat in profile. The sides are uncluttered apart from chrome detailing on the door handles, the door-mirror caps, and the proudly worn V8 badge.

A couple of very useful innovations should smooth Nissan's debut in a previously untapped sector. The load bed comes complete with a factory-installed spray-in bed liner to protect it from scratches and eventual corrosion. Also, the Titan has no B-pillars, so when both doors are open there is easy access to all the interior space.

Inside, the cab is spacious and straightforward, with clearly laid-out controls. The door handles, knobs, and assist grips are all designed specifically for the Titan, and can be used with work gloves on; it's a small detail, and more costly for Nissan than picking existing car-like components out of its enormous parts bin, but it will definitely please Titan users.

# Opel GTC Genève

"GTC" stands for Gran Turismo Compact and is a fashionable enough abbreviation, Opel hopes, to make us believe that it has discovered an all-new vehicle segment. This concept car is, in fact, a three-door coupé and so isn't a novelty; in 1999 Opel's American cousin Saturn put a three-door coupé, the SC2, on sale in the USA. Even so, it's new for Europe, and Opel could claim that the GTC Genève's large-car underpinnings give it the ride qualities to justify its grand name.

The exterior design language uses taut lines, uninterrupted surfaces, wide wheel arches, and strong features—all already seen in studies such as the Snowtrekker and in production models such as the Speedster and the Vectra.

With new dynamic design language, the GTC Genève appears to mix design elements from other makes, like the centerline feature on the front bumper and hood, the small rear quarter-light, and the strong C-pillar—all reminiscent of Renault. This car looks individual, but it's really following the design fashions of today rather than forging them.

A tinted, transparent roof, stretching from the windshield to the rear window, lies on top of a curved roofline that creates a powerful tension that is visible from the side. The clear headlights and tail lights are jewel-like, and mounted centrally above the rear window are two rather overdesigned brake lights.

The interior is sporty, with upholstery of cashmere and brown leather. The cockpit has charcoal-colored surfaces, and some even darker ones, to give the lie to the modern cliché that aluminum best suggests sportiness.

| Design | Martin Smith and Friedhelm Engler |
|---|---|
| Front tyres | 245/40R19 |
| Rear tyres | 245/40R19 |
| Length | 4349 mm (171.2 in.) |
| Width | 1773 mm (69.8 in.) |
| Height | 1352 mm (53.2 in.) |

# Opel Meriva

| Design | Friedhelm Engler |
| --- | --- |
| Engine | 1.8 in-line 4 (1.6 in-line 4 and 1.7 in-line 4 diesel also offered) |
| Power | 92 kW (123 bhp) |
| Torque | 165 Nm (122 lb. ft) @ 4600 rpm |
| Gearbox | Easytronic |
| Installation | Front-engined/front-wheel drive |
| Front suspension | MacPherson strut |
| Rear suspension | Torsion-crank axle |
| Brakes front/rear | Discs/discs, ABS, BA |
| Front tyres | 185/60R15 |
| Rear tyres | 185/60R15 |
| Length | 4040 mm (159.1 in.) |
| Width | 1694 mm (66.7 in.) |
| Height | 1620 mm (63.8 in.) |
| Wheelbase | 2630 mm (167.3 in.) |

In 2003, the new Meriva will not replace Opel's—or, in the UK, Vauxhall's—mainstay MPV, the Zafira, but will instead complement its big brother as an ultracompact people-carrier. It relates to the Corsa in the same way that the Zafira shares some engineering with the Vauxhall Astra, and will be built alongside the Corsa at the Zaragoza plant, in Spain, for Europe. The other source will be San José dos Campos, in Brazil, for the South American market, where it will be called the Chevrolet Meriva; General Motors always likes to extract as much from each new vehicle as possible.

A five-seater minivan, rather smaller than the Zafira, the Meriva is quite understated and inoffensive, despite being curvy, with short body overhangs, and curved roof pillars that continue over to the rear pillars. The overall proportions are of a cab-forward design with a curved back, like a scaled-down Citroën Picasso. A rising feature line runs from the headlights right to the rear, creating dynamic shoulders that portray strength.

The established Opel face is more prominent now, with a chrome band across the trapezoidal grille carrying the lightning-flash motif, while the tail lights sit neatly in the pillars alongside the rear screen.

Inside, the color scheme is dark gray. The main design objective, however, was the backseat concept, a folding system that turns the rear passenger area into a flat-floored cargo space that would not shame a small delivery van.

Available as an option are so-called "infotainment" systems providing information, music, and video. In the Meriva, this translates as in-car navigation, a car phone, or the OnStar telematics service.

Opel believes that this low-cost minivan will, by 2005, have taken a considerable share of a half-million-unit market segment. On this basis, GM is playing pretty safe with its design execution.

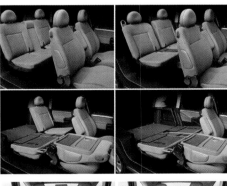

# Opel Signum

The new Opel Signum is bold in very many ways. The overall proportions are strongly biased toward the rear end, with a long and tall horizontal roofline that continues until it gives way to the forward-sloping tailgate. Initiated by the curve of the headlight, a rising waistline runs right through to the rear light and creates the car's dominant feature. A large C-pillar is chosen in place of a rear quarter-light to add to an impression of indomitable strength.

The Signum is the latest model in General Motors Europe's new lineup to display the European operation's new strong design features. These include, at the front, large, square headlights and a centerline crease; at the side, broad shoulders and chunky color-keyed features; and, at the rear, an upper glazed, inset tailgate complete with a horizontal band running below the lights. Perhaps surprisingly, the first Signum concept was revealed in 1997, so we've been waiting six years to see this car made flesh.

But there's no subtlety in this design. As a result of the striving for visual solidity, it lacks finesse, and this makes it appear too masculine. It could be described as overdesigned and, for this reason, isn't a very attractive car.

The new Vectra has been a sluggish seller to date, and Opel, together with its British sister brand Vauxhall, must hope that the added consistency in the range of the new Signum will help get people accustomed to the new look, and draw customers into showrooms. Only time will tell, but at first viewing this new model doesn't hit the mark.

| Engine | 3.0 V6 diesel (2.0 and 2.2 gasoline in-line 4 also offered) |
| --- | --- |
| Power | 132 kW (177 bhp) |
| Torque | 370 Nm (273 lb. ft) |
| Gearbox | 6-speed manual |
| Length | 4636 mm (182.5 in.) |

# Peugeot H₂O

Sometimes an unconventional idea like the H$_2$O actually makes a lot of sense. At first sight, this is simply a whimsical concept for a compact fire-fighting vehicle, despite Peugeot's assertion that the H$_2$O was designed in conjunction with French firemen so that it can, uniquely, fit into tight spaces inaccessible to conventional fire engines.

But look more closely and the true rationale for the H$_2$O concept becomes apparent: it is a showcase for future fuel-cell technology. The H$_2$O is an electric vehicle fitted with batteries and an auxiliary power unit in the form of a fuel cell, the function of which is to provide a permanent supply of electrical energy to power emergency equipment.

To operate, a fuel cell requires hydrogen and oxygen. Oxygen is drawn from the air or from a bottle, whereas the hydrogen must be produced on board when needed. The H$_2$O, notionally, retains all its functions when in an anaerobic (without oxygen) environment—for instance, when there is a fire in a tunnel or an underground car park. In this case, the oxygen necessary for the fuel cell is supplied from two bottles carried on the vehicle.

At the rear of the two-person passenger compartment are a water tank, a telescopic ladder across the top, various storage compartments, an assortment of sockets and connections, and blue flashing beacons—all vital for tackling a blaze.

At the front, the large air intake, for cooling the electric motor and brakes, is prominent. The headlight design is rectilinear and shares its style with those on last year's sporty RC concepts.

The interior displays a modern, functional dashboard that groups together various controls. As one would expect, it is red, and it has a few metal finishing touches that are also found around the side vents. At the top are a touch screen, a telephone, and a GPS system. In front of the passenger is a second screen, linked to a PC that can display maps of large buildings.

Clearly, the H$_2$O's elaborate premise would be of little practical use in a major emergency, and fire-fighters would take a dim view of such frivolity. Still, some promise lies behind this cartoonish device.

| Design | Gerard Welter |
| --- | --- |
| Front tyres | 215/45R18 |
| Rear tyres | 215/45R18 |
| Length | 4294 mm (169.1 in.) |
| Width | 1689 mm (66.5 in.) |
| Height | 1679 mm (66.1 in.) |
| Wheelbase | 2690 mm (105.9 in.) |
| Track front/rear | 1566/1566 mm (61.7/61.7 in.) |
| Curb weight | 1700 kg (3748 lb.) |

# Peugeot Hoggar

| | |
|---|---|
| Design | Somvang Sinhsattanak |
| Engine | Two 2.2 in-line 4 Hdi units |
| Power | 268 kW (360 bhp) |
| Torque | 800 Nm (590 lb. ft) |
| Gearbox | 6-speed semi-automatic |
| Installation | Front- and rear-mounted/all-wheel drive |
| Front suspension | Double wishbone |
| Rear suspension | Double wishbone |
| Brakes front/rear | Discs/discs |
| Front tires | 21 in. |
| Rear tires | 21 in. |
| Length | 3960 mm (155.9 in.) |
| Width | 2000 mm (78.7 in.) |
| Height | 1490 mm (58.7 in.) |
| Wheelbase | 2750 mm (108.3 in.) |
| Curb weight | 1300 kg (2866 lb.) |

The Hoggar is essentially a very high-performance dune buggy designed to carry two fun-lovers.

The hood's front envelops the grille and the lion badge, while its rear end extends into the passenger compartment by means of dual rounded sections that pass through the windshield to form the two instrument pods. The radiators are set well back at windshield level to minimize the front overhang, useful to maximize the front ramp angle when off-road. Catlike headlights and a "pouncing" poise give the Hoggar an animal-like character.

Inside, there is extensive use of aluminum and leather—in particular, two structural light-alloy seats padded and covered with hide. A console-mounted touch screen controls the GPS satellite navigation system, the speedometer, and the inclinometer, and also features the obligatory MP3 player.

The Hoggar is designed as an open-air vehicle with no roof. The doors are no more than two small panels that offer little protection, and they form part of the front wings, beneath which the ground can easily be seen.

Camera technology on board doesn't extend to the rearview mirrors, but a front-mounted camera warns of obstacles when the driver is parking, and proximity detectors are also fitted.

The unfortunate thing about this type of car is that most of the time there just aren't enough potential buyers for what is essentially a grown-up's toy. The manufacturers have seldom been able to justify making them, especially as most components need to be custom-made. What a shame!

# Peugeot Sésame

| Design | Gerard Welter |
|---|---|
| Engine | 1.6 in-line 4 |
| Power | 80 kW (107 bhp) |
| Gearbox | 5-speed manual |
| Front suspension | MacPherson strut |
| Brakes front/rear | Discs/discs |
| Front tyres | R17 |
| Rear tyres | R17 |
| Length | 3700 mm (145.7 in.) |
| Width | 1670 mm (65.8 in.) |
| Height | 1630 mm (64.2 in.) |
| Wheelbase | 2310 mm (90.9 in.) |

Peugeot has enjoyed massive success in the past decade with B-segment models such as the 205 and 206, yet it is smart enough to keep researching potential new ideas for the market. The Sésame is a mono-volume design for small-car buyers in the sub-B-market segment, who might like the advantages that sliding doors offer. Mercedes-Benz has already realized a market exists here, and recently launched the Vaneo, based on the A-Class. But the Sésame is smaller than the Vaneo and has just a single sliding door to provide good access to the four individual seats.

The frontal design is similar to that of most recent Peugeot cars. From the edge of the ultra-short hood, the windshield leads to a glass roof complete with two metal roof bars at the edges. Between the bumpers, running around the wheel arches and along the sills, is a small step to give an athletic quality and a solid, defining edge.

To assist its action, the passenger door is guided by a pad sliding on a visible rail sited on the rear wing. This then joins a feature line that continues around the rear of the car, stopping at the spare-wheel cover. At the corners, this rail separates the top part, shaped by the side window which connects with the rear screen, and the base, giving the rear-light cluster its own unique shape.

The Sésame is painted in a simple, luminous yellow with a matching interior of yellow and dark blue. Depending on Peugeot's courage in probing new markets—not something the company is renowned for—the Sésame could be very close to its upcoming sub-B production offering.

# Pininfarina Enjoy

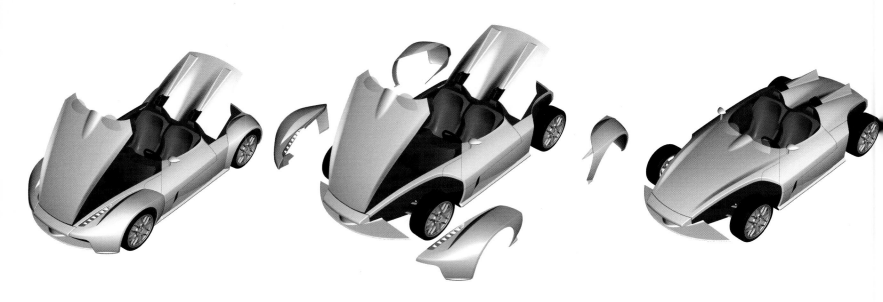

| Engine | 1.8 in-line 4 |
|---|---|
| Power | 101 kW (135 bhp) |
| Gearbox | 5-speed manual |
| Installation | Mid-engined/rear-wheel drive |
| Front suspension | Double wishbone with push-rod |
| Rear suspension | Double wishbone |
| Brakes front/rear | Discs/discs |
| Front tires | 215/40R17 |
| Rear tires | 235/40R18 |
| Length | 3740 mm (147.2 in.) |
| Width | 1790 mm (70.5 in.) |
| Height | 1070 mm (42.1 in.) |
| Wheelbase | 2375 mm (93.5 in.) |
| Track front/rear | 1525/1545 mm (60/60.8 in.) |
| Curb weight | 750 kg (1653 lb.) |

No company anywhere has better credentials than Pininfarina to design a car like the Enjoy roadster. It has a history of designing Ferraris dating back to 1952, and has also created many other outstanding concept small sports cars, including the Autobianchi A112 Giovani Spider in 1973, the Peugeot 104 Peugette Spider in 1976, the Ethos in 1992, and, more recently, Ford's Streetka (see p. 110).

Conceived for both everyday use and racing, the Enjoy is an easygoing, fun car targeted at young people who don't care much about vehicle refinement or superfluous ornamentation.

It shares the Lotus Elise's aluminum platform and, as a result, gives a drive that echoes many of that car's lightning-fast responses. That simple yet thoroughly enjoyable experience of being connected with the road and the surrounding environment is perhaps similar in many ways to riding a four-wheeled motorcycle, albeit one rather more sophisticated than a quad bike. The omission of the windshield recalls the Renault Sport Spider of the 1990s; this feature is replaced by two wind deflectors to minimize drag and exaggerate the "hard-core" open-air motoring experience.

Reflecting the same philosophy, the cockpit is extremely simple. The seats and trim are produced from fireproof and waterproof materials, again as in a motorbike. The controls and instruments are also very basic and there is nothing decorative or complicated about the dashboard—in fact, it's almost non-existent. The steering wheel is shaped to facilitate getting into the driving seat and is fitted with its own engine rev counter for track driving.

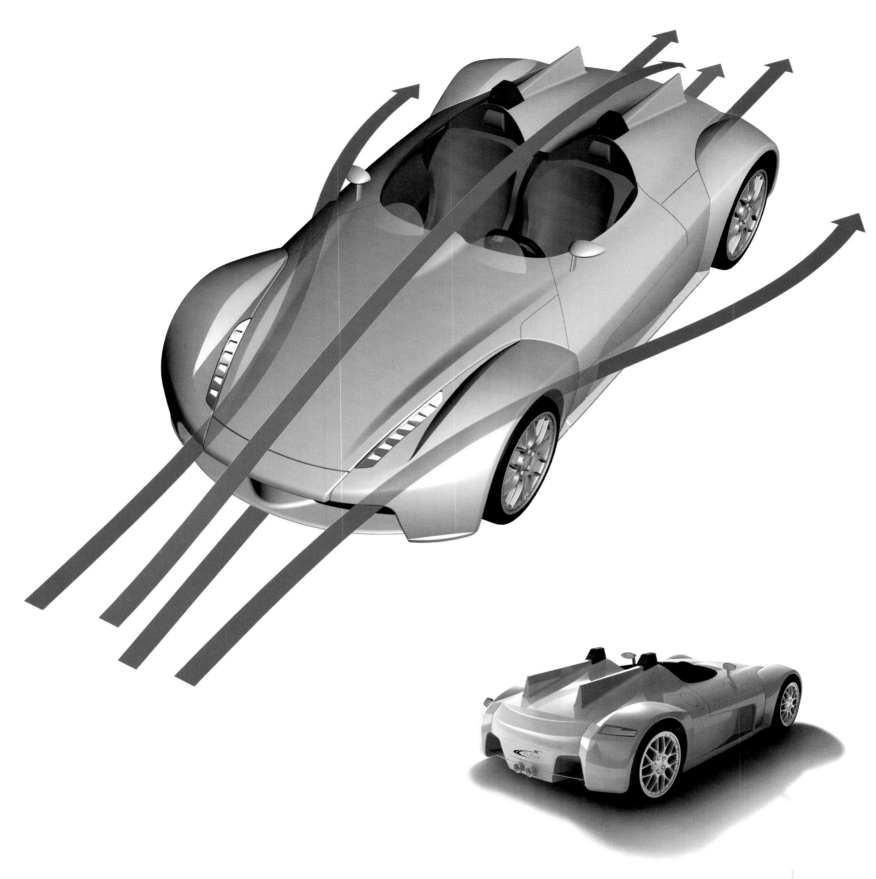

# Pontiac G6

| | |
|---|---|
| Design | Tim Kozub |
| Engine | 3.5 V6 supercharged |
| Power | 213 kW (286 bhp) |
| Torque | 369 Nm (272 lb. ft) |
| Gearbox | 4-speed automatic |
| Installation | Front-engined/all-wheel drive |
| Brakes front/rear | Discs/discs |
| Front tires | 245/40ZR20 |
| Rear tires | 245/40ZR20 |
| Length | 4679 mm (184.2 in.) |
| Width | 1778 mm (70 in.) |
| Height | 1321 mm (52 in.) |
| Wheelbase | 2873 mm (113.1 in.) |
| Track front/rear | 1618/1626mm (63.7/64 in.) |
| Curb weight | 1501 kg (3309 lb.) |

A four-seater GT car from Pontiac is a revived idea for the brand—after all, the 1960s and 1970s glory days of the fire-breathing GTO are a distant memory. With a wedge-shaped stance and pumped-up body language, the G6 is a powerful statement about Pontiac's performance ambitions for the future.

At the front, the distinctive Pontiac grille sits within the molded bumper, in a similar way to the Solstice concept shown a year ago. The high-intensity LED headlights and indicators are incorporated in the same unit and form the start of the hood feature line, and, more significantly, the wedge that runs through to the rear lights. The effect is to give the car its highly dynamic stance.

The G6 is designed to be a sophisticated GT rather than an outright sports car. The smooth surfaces have been crafted to be uncluttered and easy on the eye. Proportionally, the overhangs are short, and the car is wide and low, signifying its dynamic road behavior. The powertrain can switch into the "Displacement on Demand" mode, in which, during routine driving conditions, half of the cylinders are deactivated and saved for more powerful and demanding situations.

Inside the G6, the look is of technical sophistication and driver orientation. Titanium bezels and other trimmings on the center console and doors combine with blue and maroon leather. This is a color scheme some might find cold and unwelcoming, but the overall impression is of a quality car.

# Pontiac Grand Prix

| Design | John Manoogian |
|---|---|
| Engine | 3.8 V6 supercharged |
| Power | 194 kW (260 bhp) @ 5200 rpm |
| Torque | 380 Nm (280 lb. ft) @ 3600 rpm |
| Gearbox | 4-speed automatic |
| Installation | Front-engined/front-wheel drive |
| Front suspension | MacPherson strut |
| Rear suspension | Tri-link |
| Brakes front/rear | Discs/discs, ABS |
| Front tires | P225/55R17 |
| Rear tires | P225/55R17 |
| Length | 5035 mm (198 in.) |
| Width | 1819 mm (71.6 in.) |
| Height | 1420 mm (55.9 in.) |
| Wheelbase | 2807 mm (110.5 in.) |
| Track front/rear | 1567/1545 mm (61.7/60.8 in.) |
| Curb weight | 1581 kg (3486 lb.) |
| 0–100 km/h (62 mph) | 6.5 sec |
| Top speed | 174 km/h (108 mph) |
| Fuel consumption | 10.7 ltr/100 km (22 mpg) |

Since the debut of the first Pontiac Grand Prix, in 1962, this midsized model has always been a car with a sporty flavor, as its name suggests. In its modernity, the latest Grand Prix presents Pontiac's new design direction.

The car is sleek. It has a curved nose and a sportiness that radiates directly from it; the distinctive grille sets up the three feature lines that rise up over the hood and outward toward the A-pillars. Large spotlights are positioned far outboard on the bumper, which rises in the center to make way for a lower spoiler. This is set back, a position which probably has an aerodynamic purpose but also visually lightens the weight at the front end.

From the side, the profile is a long wedge that incorporates the coupé-style roofline, rear screen, and rear-door window glass. As the C-pillars twist inboard, a shelf gradually emerges along the rear door and leads on to the trunk lid's surface, and then to the rear spoiler. Because the rear screen is narrow and the triangular tail lights are large, the trunk lid opening is compromised.

Inside is a contrast to the exciting exterior: the fabrics and leather are gray and uninspiring. Masses of circular air vents, and a cluttered look, may frustrate consumers accustomed to other manufacturers' more appealing interiors. But the Grand Prix does come with a head-up display that features a "stealth" mode, letting the driver navigate from it with the instrument cluster's lights off.

# Porsche Cayenne

| | |
|---|---|
| Engine | 4.5 V8 turbo (4.5 V8 non-turbo also offered) |
| Power | 331 kW (444 bhp) @ 6000 rpm |
| Torque | 620 Nm (457 lb. ft) @ 2250–4750 rpm |
| Gearbox | 6-speed Tiptronic |
| Installation | Front-engined/4-wheel drive |
| Front suspension | Double-track control arms |
| Rear suspension | Multi-arm axle |
| Brakes front/rear | Discs/discs, ABS |
| Front tires | 255/55R18 |
| Rear tires | 255/55R18 |
| Length | 4786 mm (188.3 in.) |
| Width | 1928 mm (75.9 in.) |
| Height | 1699 mm (66.9 in.) |
| Wheelbase | 2855 mm (112.4 in.) |
| Track front/rear | 1647/1662 mm (64.8/65.4 in.) |
| Curb weight | 2355 kg (5192 lb.) |
| 0–100 km/h (62 mph) | 5.6 sec |
| Top speed | 266 km/h (165 mph) |
| Fuel consumption | 15.7 ltr/100 km (15 mpg) |
| $CO_2$ emissions | 378 g/km |

The new Cayenne is a landmark in Porsche's history. After the company's exclusive concentration on dedicated sports cars, this latest collaboration with Volkswagen (previous ones, such as the VW–Porsche 914/6 and Volkswagen-engined Porsche 924, have been sports cars too) lets Porsche enter a completely new market sector. The strength of the German Porsche brand, with its unsullied sporting pedigree, is a much-envied legend within the car industry. Also, this is a brand that many people aspire to. So Porsche hopes these two factors will help win lucrative sales for its new SUV.

It was always going to be a challenge to style the Cayenne. Achieving styling coherence is vitally important, to ensure that Porsche's heritage is instantly recognizable. And the task was made even harder by the fact that the Cayenne's platform and center section, even down to its door handles, are shared with the Volkswagen Touareg.

Building in key Porsche styling features has mostly been achieved; the low, inset, sloping "V" hood, triangular, swept-back headlights, flared wheel arches, and tapered body at the rear are good examples. Even so, proportions intrinsic to the iconic 911 naturally clash with those found on SUVs, which are normally square and rugged, especially at the front. The Cayenne is lighter at the front, maybe more feminine, and the rear is completely new territory for Porsche: totally devoted to SUV practicality and impossible to imbue with any genuine Porsche hallmarks.

So what is the result? Not very dissimilar from the Volkswagen Touareg (see p. 238), obviously, albeit using Porsche surface language. The fact is, this is—visually—the most compromised Porsche ever.

The interior looks well made, with two-tone leather split by aluminum beading running around the cabin to give a sporty, technical edge. In front of the driver, the large instruments clearly display all the necessary information.

This car will sell, no doubt well and certainly profitably. A race-bred heritage could be contrived for it too, possibly on events such as the infamously tough Paris–Dakar. But, in terms of design, the Cayenne has left many critics cold.

# Renault Ellypse

| Design | Patrick le Quément |
|---|---|
| Engine | 1.2 in-line 4 turbo-diesel |
| Power | 72 kW (97 bhp) |
| Torque | 200 Nm (147 lb. ft) |
| Gearbox | 5-speed robotized/shift-by-wire |
| Installation | Front-engined/front-wheel drive |
| Front tires | 19 in. PAX run-flat system |
| Rear tires | 19 in. PAX run-flat system |
| Length | 3930 mm (154.7 in.) |
| Width | 1770 mm (69.7 in.) |
| Height | 1520 mm (59.9 in.) |
| Wheelbase | 2610 mm (102.8 in.) |
| Track front/rear | 1595/1595 mm (62.8/62.8 in.) |
| Curb weight | 980 kg (2160 lb.) |
| Fuel consumption | 3.2 ltr/100 km (73.5 mpg) |
| CO$_2$ emissions | 85 g/km |

The excitement of the Paris Motor Show every two years is always partly due to the suspense of seeing what Renault will reveal. And in 2002 it was the Ellypse concept, a monospace with softly structured modern surfaces, two-tone coloring—blue-tinted almond for the front and rear, and ultra-light blue for the doors—and a face and tail design that sit comfortably with Renault's brand identity. Its horizontal proportions and similar feature lines, together with bold arcs, give it a friendly feel.

While the left side is equipped with traditional doors, the right has an innovative two-way opening system. There is no B-pillar: the rear door either opens as a classic swing door, to give direct access to the rear seats, or tilts from front to back.

The interior is minimalist, with the shape of the dashboard leading on to the floor to create a gentle wave that supports the four seats. The dashboard also adopts a streamlined design, with two central displays neatly summarizing essential data. One shows driving information, while the other displays "passenger information" and can be folded away.

The Ellypse's interior utilizes the "Touch Design" concept first seen on the Talisman concept in 2001. Touch Design is basically a series of simple shapes and "technology hubs" grouping the different driver functions. The idea is to make controls and functions intuitively easy and pleasant to use.

In addition, the Ellypse explores new ways to make components from recycled materials, particularly for the soundproofing, which is made mainly from cotton from old clothing, and with polyester fibers from pre-sorted plastic bottles and packaging.

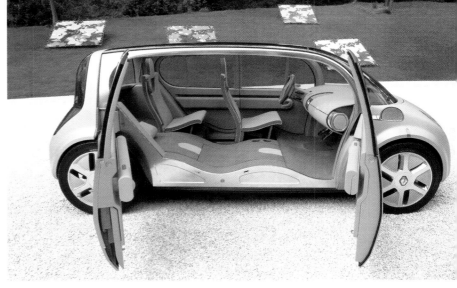

# Renault Espace

| | |
|---|---|
| Design | Patrick le Quément |
| Engine | 3.5 V6 (1.9 and 2.2 in-line 4 turbo-diesel, and 3.0 V6 turbo-diesel, also offered) |
| Power | 177 kW (245 bhp) @ 6000 rpm |
| Torque | 330 Nm (243 lb. ft) @ 3600 rpm |
| Gearbox | 5-speed manual |
| Installation | Front-engined/front-wheel drive |
| Front suspension | MacPherson strut |
| Rear suspension | Torsion beam |
| Brakes front/rear | Discs/discs, ABS, EBD |
| Front tires | 225/55R17 |
| Rear tires | 225/55R17 |
| Length | 4661 mm (183.5 in.) |
| Width | 1860 mm (73.2 in.) |
| Height | 1728 mm (68 in.) |
| Wheelbase | 2803 mm (110.4 in.) |
| Track front/rear | 1574/1556 mm (62/61.3 in.) |
| Curb weight | 1815 kg (4001 lb.) |
| 0–100 km/h (62 mph) | 8.1 sec |
| Top speed | 225 km/h (140 mph) |
| Fuel consumption | 12.4 ltr/100 km (19 mpg) |
| $CO_2$ emissions | 297 g/km |

The fourth version in the evolution of Renault's Espace has set its sights further upmarket. Following in the design footsteps of the Vel Satis and Avantime, the new car is a large, sleek monospace, like the previous one, but with sportier, more masculine lines. As before, the Espace and the longer-wheelbase Grand Espace are offered.

At the front, the headlights underline the streamlined shape, and the enormous windshield gives excellent all-round vision. The Espace has the largest production glass roof in the world, at 2.16 square meters (23.3 sq ft), and this allows floods of natural light to illuminate the cabin. It is all a long way from the utilitarian passenger box that impressed everyone twenty years ago.

The cabin is elegant and, says Renault, draws its inspiration from contemporary architecture and furniture. This can be taken to mean the classier, more minimalist end of the domestic domain. The sculpted and unfussy dashboard has a satin finish extending outward to the door panels. For the dashboard, textiles have been abandoned in favor of a slush finish, to give a serene, restful atmosphere. The upper section is slightly darker, emphasizing the technology imbedded inside.

No cheap sofas here: traditional velour is replaced with woven fabrics for a neater appearance and a more pleasing touch. The seat material incorporates a thread with a contrasting appearance that, when combined with alcantara, gives a dry, soft feel. It is this sort of detail that makes the interior particularly inviting and tactile. The rear of the car, with its boosted elbow- and head-room, has been redesigned solely with greater comfort for rear passengers in mind.

Technology enhancements are also a given, and these include an automatic parking brake, the Carminat navigation system with foldaway screen, parking proximity sensors, rain and light sensors, and a gas tank flap with an intriguing built-in cap. Then there is the credit-card-sized Renault Card, which the driver inserts into a reader to start the vehicle. This card also automatically opens and closes the windows and locks the doors.

# Renault Mégane

| | |
|---|---|
| Design | Patrick le Quément |
| Engine | 2.0 in-line 4 (1.4 and1.6 in-line 4, and 1.5 and 1.9 in-line 4 turbo-diesel, also offered) |
| Power | 98 kW (131 bhp) @ 5500 rpm |
| Torque | 191 Nm (141 lb. ft) @ 3750 rpm |
| Gearbox | 6-speed manual |
| Installation | Front-engined/front-wheel drive |
| Front suspension | MacPherson strut |
| Rear suspension | Torsion beam |
| Brakes front/rear | Discs/discs EBD, ESP |
| Front tires | 205/55R16 |
| Rear tires | 205/55R16 |
| Length | 4209 mm (165.7 in.) |
| Width | 1777 mm (70 in.) |
| Height | 1457 mm (57.4 in.) |
| Wheelbase | 2625 mm (103.3 in.) |
| Track front/rear | 1510/1506 mm (59.4/59.3 in.) |
| Curb weight | 1250 kg (2756 lb.) |
| 0–100 km/h (62 mph) | 9.2 sec |
| Top speed | 200 km/h (124 mph) |
| Fuel consumption | 8 ltr/100 km (29.4 mpg) |
| CO$_2$ emissions | 191 g/km |

Renault's new Mégane II adds another piece to its jigsaw of new visual identity, which includes the larger Vel Satis and late-lamented Avantime. Sitting in the family-car C-segment, the Mégane II is a distinctive ship in a sea of mostly mediocre design, since most of its many competitors look pretty much the same. That goes for the outgoing Mégane models too: apart from the Mégane Scénic, the three- and five-door cars were at best competent.

The Mégane II's exterior is unique, particularly at its extremities. At the front, the theme is angular, with three air intakes that split the bumper. The centerline spine remains and the edge of the hood flares to create a much higher wing line compared with that of the previous model. At the rear, the theme follows the Avantime, with a vertical drop off the roof, while the trunk bulges outward.

Instruments and dials are grouped in two deeply hooded binnacles: these two humps and the cylindrical dial housings look like the instruments found on powerful motorbikes, and are another pleasingly sexy touch for the emasculated family man at the wheel.

The Mégane II is the first volume-produced car to feature "Touch Design," design chief Patrick le Quément's principle by which the driver's controls must suggest their function, and are shaped and positioned accordingly for maximum ease of use. If you ponder that description, you could be forgiven for thinking it could have applied to just about any car, ever. But, if it helps to sell stimulating design to the mass car market, then we must take it at face value.

While Renault must be congratulated on breaking many molds with its latest cars, the Mégane II will have to sell more strongly than the Vel Satis for the spicy new visual identity to be acclaimed a real success.

# Renault Scénic 2

| | |
|---|---|
| Design | Patrick le Quément |
| Engine | 2.0 in-line 4 (1.4, 1.5, and 1.6 in-line 4, and 1.9 in-line 4 diesel, also offered) |
| Power | 101 kW (136 bhp) @ 5500 rpm |
| Torque | 191 Nm (141 lb. ft) @ 3750 rpm |
| Gearbox | 6-speed manual |
| Installation | Front-engined/front-wheel drive |
| Front suspension | MacPherson strut |
| Rear suspension | Torsion beam |
| Brakes front/rear | Discs/discs, ABS, BA |
| Front tires | 205/60R16 |
| Rear tires | 205/60R16 |
| Length | 4250 mm (178 in.) |
| Width | 1805 mm (71 in.) |
| Height | 1620 mm (63.8 in.) |
| Wheelbase | 2685 mm (105.7 in.) |
| Track front/rear | 1506/1506 mm (59.3/59.3 in.) |
| Curb weight | 1400 kg (3086 lb.) |
| 0–100 km/h (62 mph) | 10.5 sec |
| Top speed | 195 km/h (121 mph) |
| Fuel consumption | 8 ltr/100 km (29.4 mpg) |
| CO$_2$ emissions | 192 g/km |

Here is the replacement for one of the landmark cars of the late twentieth century—a car we didn't know we wanted until it arrived. The first Renault Mégane Scénic went on to prove a resilient benchmark for the C segment, despite an onslaught of competitors, and has sold over two million units since it was introduced in 1997.

The design community fully expected that the new model would come with large headlights and a dark grille at the front, plus, to match the design language of recent arrivals in the company's lineup, a stepped-out trunk. It has these, but it also shares some aspects with the Ellypse concept, particularly in its overall proportions.

However, the strong arch feature of the side windows, the two-tone paint, and the wacky interior have been dropped for a more traditional setup. Exciting though it was, the Ellypse was probably just too futuristic to be translated unaltered for today's market.

The Scénic 2 has some new features in addition to those of the model it replaces, such as an automatic parking brake, bi-xenon headlights, and a gas-tank flap with built-in cap. Increased storage space and better personal safety are offered, too.

Relaxing hues and gentle curves make the interior welcoming. Mounted centrally on the dashboard, the instrument panel is visible to every occupant. The Renault-branded "Touch Design" treatment is prominent in the controls and is intended to make their use more intuitive and pleasant. The large panoramic sunroof provides natural light throughout the car.

The original Scénic was voted European Car of the Year in 1997 and has definitely left its mark on the segment. This new model should also serve Renault well.

# Rinspeed Bedouin

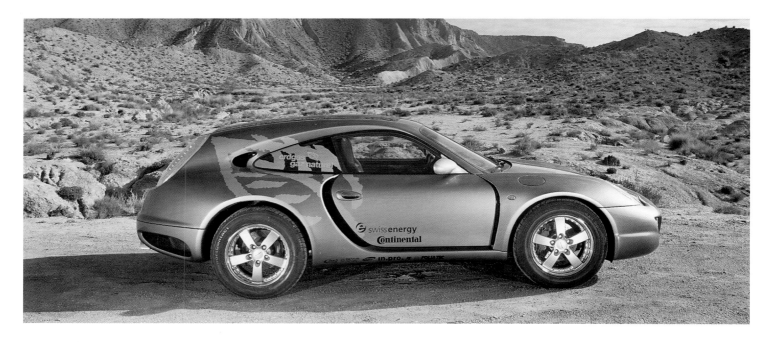

| Design | Thomas Clever |
|---|---|
| Engine | 3.6 horizontally opposed six-cylinder |
| Power | 313 kW (420 bhp) @ 6000 rpm |
| Torque | 560 Nm (413 lb. ft) @ 2700 rpm |
| Gearbox | 6-speed manual |
| Installation | Rear-engined/4-wheel drive |
| Brakes front/rear | Discs/discs |
| Front tires | 255/55R18 |
| Rear tires | 285/50R18 |
| Length | 4458 mm (175.5 in.) |
| Width | 1975 mm (77.8 in.) |
| Height | 1458 mm (57.4 in.) |
| Wheelbase | 2350 mm (92.5 in.) |
| Track front/rear | 1562/1675 mm (61.5/65.9 in.) |
| Curb weight | 1640 kg (3616 lb.) |
| 0–100 km/h (62 mph) | 5.9 sec |
| Top speed | 250 km/h (155 mph) limited |

The new Rinspeed Bedouin can be transformed from a pickup to a four-seater SUV in about ten seconds. The front part of the roof folds and, in effect, becomes the tailgate window, while the rear part of the roof turns into the cargo bay. Rinspeed, a German customizing company that usually stuns visitors to motor shows with its outlandish designs, claims the tailgate can be lowered to extend the bay, which can then be used to transport bulky goods. Alternatively, the enlarged bay can serve as the base for a modern tent—hence the name "Bedouin."

Aesthetically, the Bedouin is a disaster. Largely based on the Porsche 996 platform and sharing many components, it tries in vain to combine powerful Porsche surfaces with a heavy, stuck-on rear end that totally upsets the car's balance. From the rear, the strakes running down the rear window and over the roof look completely out of place among the otherwise curvaceous forms of the rest of the car.

In the Bedouin, Rinspeed has worked with other companies to investigate future technologies. This is where the concept gets more interesting. For example, the Bedouin runs on natural gas and is, in fact, the fastest car on earth to be powered by the stuff.

The crystal manufacturer Swarovski helped create the gearshift grip, made from solid crystal. The Rinspeed logos shimmer in gold and are inset with the tiniest crystals. Magpies would love them. However, Rinspeed should leave designing to the professionals and concentrate instead on technological innovations, at which it might excel.

# Rolls-Royce Phantom

| | |
|---|---|
| Design | Marek Djordjevic |
| Engine | 6.7 V12 |
| Power | 338 kW (453 bhp) @ 5350 rpm |
| Torque | 720 Nm (531 lb. ft) @ 3500 rpm |
| Gearbox | 6-speed automatic |
| Installation | Front-engined/rear-wheel drive |
| Front suspension | Double wishbone |
| Rear suspension | Multi-link |
| Brakes front/rear | Discs/discs |
| Front tires | PAX 265 × 790 R540 A/S |
| Rear tires | PAX 265 × 790 R540 A/S |
| Length | 5834 mm (229.7 in.) |
| Width | 1990 mm (78.3 in.) |
| Height | 1632 mm (64.3 in.) |
| Wheelbase | 3570 mm (140.6 in.) |
| Curb weight | 2530 kg (5577 lb.) |
| 0–100 km/h (62 mph) | 5.9 sec |
| Top speed | 240 km/h (149 mph) |
| Fuel consumption | 15.9 ltr/100 km (14.8 mpg) |

Since BMW gained the rights to Rolls-Royce, in July 1998, it has been busy setting up a brand-new company, with new headquarters at Goodwood in the UK. Five years later it has finally taken the brand over from its caretaker owner, Volkswagen, after Rolls-Royce was painfully split from its longtime partner make, Bentley.

During that time, BMW has decided to abandon the unloved Silver Seraph and drop the slow-selling Corniche convertible, and has carefully planned the entirely new Phantom model from scratch. It has taken the German car giant four and a half years to bring this modern interpretation of a classic Rolls-Royce to the marketplace, and it's no coincidence that it was first shown in the USA—its key market.

Although its V12 engine comes from Germany, most of the car's parts are manufactured in the UK using cutting-edge technology and skilled craftsmanship drawn from the yacht-building industry local to the new West Sussex factory. For the first time a Rolls-Royce is built on an aluminum platform, making it fundamentally new throughout. The lack of B-pillars, together with the use of rear-hinged rear doors, allows complete open access to the interior when both doors are open.

For inspiration, the designers looked at the Phantom I and II models of the 1920s, the Phantom III from the 1930s, the Silver Cloud from the 1950s, and the Silver Shadow from the 1960s. Design elements have been transferred to the new Phantom: a long wheelbase, deep C-pillars, and a long hood. The stance and proportion of the Phantom, Rolls claims, make it look like it's moving even when stationary.

The luxurious interior employs fine leather, cashmere trim, and hand-crafted wood to create the expected atmosphere of quality and serenity. A few special details are worth a mention because they will delight owners and onlookers alike: the electrically retractable Spirit of Ecstasy radiator mascot, which can be lowered out of sight whenever the Phantom is parked; the wheel hub centers complete with double-R logos that remain upright at all times; and umbrellas stowed within each rear door.

# Saab 9-3

| Design | Michael Mauer |
|---|---|
| Engine | 2.0 in-line 4 (2.1 in-line 4 diesel also offered) |
| Power | 155 kW (208 bhp) @ 5300 rpm |
| Torque | 300 Nm (221 lb. ft) @ 2500 rpm |
| Gearbox | 6-speed manual |
| Installation | Front-engined/front-wheel drive |
| Front suspension | MacPherson strut |
| Rear suspension | Independent 4-link |
| Brakes front/rear | Discs/discs, ABS, TCS, BA |
| Length | 4635 mm (182.5 in.) |
| Width | 1762 mm (69.4 in.) |
| Height | 1466 mm (57.7 in.) |
| Wheelbase | 2675 mm (105.3 in.) |
| Track front/rear | 1524/1506 mm (60/59.3 in.) |
| Curb weight | 1500 kg (3307 lb.) |
| 0–100 km/h (62 mph) | 7.5 sec |
| Top speed | 235 km/h (146 mph) |
| Fuel consumption | 8.5 ltr/100 km (27.7 mpg) |

Saab's new 9-3 is a sporty, coupé-like executive sedan with the sort of look of strength we have come to expect from the Swedish brand. The new car is 50 mm (2 in.) wider and about 75 mm (3 in.) longer than the previous 9-3, which gives it a more purposeful stance. Aerodynamics appear to have had a high development priority; the shape at the front is gently raked, leading to the wraparound windshield, and then across the roof to the tapered rear windshield and on to the trunk spoiler.

Saab's design DNA reassuringly runs throughout, examples being the wraparound windshield, the teardrop form of the side windows with a disguised B-pillar, the wedge shape, and the high waistline culminating in the distinctive "hockey stick" curve into the C-pillar. A single swage line runs the entire length of the car and, of course, those prominent oval-shaped door handles stand out.

Inside, everything is conventional and classic, with soft curves and functional black and white switches and buttons. The interior comes in either "light room" (parchment) or "dark room" (gray) tones, the latter being slightly more sporty because it sets off the aluminum detailing more distinctively.

A detail maybe, but Saab has a widely reported feature on its 9-5 model: its cupholder complete with a highly complex mechanism. For the 9-3, a new one was designed, called the "Butterfly." This has two separate movements in different directions, one for the base and one for the retaining hoop (together these are the butterfly's "wings"), which are both hinged from one arm. A highly geared action makes the wings open and close as the arm moves in and out. At least the feature is something genuinely novel in this otherwise gently evolving model.

# Saturn Ion

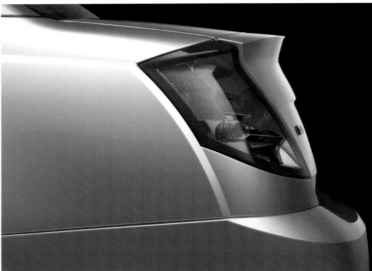

| Design | Tim Greig |
|---|---|
| Engine | 2.2 in-line 4 |
| Power | 102 kW (137 bhp) @ 5600 rpm |
| Torque | 193 Nm (142 lb. ft) @ 4200 rpm |
| Gearbox | 5-speed manual, CVT or 5-speed automatic |
| Installation | Front-engined/front-wheel drive |
| Front suspension | MacPherson strut |
| Rear suspension | Semi-independent torsion beam |
| Brakes front/rear | Discs/drums |
| Front tires | 185/70R14 |
| Rear tires | 185/70R14 |
| Length | 4686 mm (184.5 in.) |
| Width | 1707 mm (67.2 in.) |
| Height | 1458 mm (57.4 in.) |
| Wheelbase | 2621 mm (103.2 in.) |
| Curb weight | 1247 kg (2750 lb.) |

Saturn's new Ion replaces the very long-running S-Series introduced back in 1991. This was the manufacturer's debut model, and has since sold more than two million cars. However, despite the fact that Saturn was a much-vaunted from-scratch project—offering a new car built and sold in new ways—the brand has been confined almost exclusively to America and has made little impact internationally.

The Ion comes as the refined-looking Sedan and the sportier Quad Coupe, both built on GM's new Delta small-car architecture and promising high levels of chassis tautness and excellent refinement. Indeed, the Ion has a solid, structural look on the outside, and although different the two models share some classic Saturn characteristics. These include the horizontal headlights, the "shark fins" at the door mirror and the back of the rear door, the upswept "swoosh" in the polymer door panels, and the embossed "SATURN" in the rear bumper.

The Quad Coupe has distinctive dual rear-access doors, which are intended to make it easy to load and unload passengers, while a highly visible feature on both models is the polymer roof trim, giving a modern impression.

Partly responsible for the Sedan's distinctive presence are the vertically shaped tail lights inset at the uppermost back corners, which bring the eye up. The rear of the Quad Coupe sits visually higher than the Sedan's, and is significantly more swept from the roofline to the trunk lid's downward bevel.

The aerodynamic profile of the Quad Coupe gives a clean, uncluttered appearance; the cowl is moved slightly forward, which adds to the windswept effect, as does a sleeker rear-end profile.

# Scion xA

| | |
|---|---|
| **Design** | Toyota Design |
| **Engine** | 1.5 in-line 4 |
| **Power** | 81 kW (108 bhp) @ 6000 rpm |
| **Torque** | 142 Nm (105 lb. ft) @ 4200 rpm |
| **Gearbox** | 5-speed manual |
| **Installation** | Front-engined/front-wheel drive |
| **Front suspension** | MacPherson strut |
| **Rear suspension** | Torsion beam |
| **Brakes front/rear** | Discs/drums, ABS |
| **Front tires** | 185/60R15 |
| **Rear tires** | 185/60R15 |
| **Length** | 3914 mm (154.1 in.) |
| **Width** | 1694 mm (66.7 in.) |
| **Height** | 1529 mm (60.2 in.) |
| **Wheelbase** | 2370 mm (93.3 in.) |
| **Track front/rear** | 1455/1430 mm (57.3/56.3 in.) |
| **Curb weight** | 1061 kg (2340 lb.) |

The Scion is a brand-new car make to be launched by Toyota, repeating the "clean sheet of paper" exercise the company did with Lexus in the early 1990s. This time, however, the brand will target the youth market and not the portly executive.

The first two new models to wear the Scion badge are the xA and xB, which were unveiled at the 2003 Greater Los Angeles Auto Show. They will initially be sold only in California, but will eventually roll out across North America.

Rather than totally new cars, the Scion models—the name means "descendant"—are an exercise in rebranding. The xA is based on the Black Box, and the xB on the bb, both cars that are currently available in Japan under the Toyota banner. But by building a new brand with Scion, Toyota hopes to target the relatively unexploited youth market in the USA.

The xA has a muscular, sporty stance, with sculpted wheel arches, a strong grille, large headlights, and strongly defined feature lines that run from front to back. The wheels look slightly too small but, in keeping with Scion's "personalization philosophy," larger wheels are sure to be available as an option.

The interior of the xA is also sporty, with mainly dark-gray panels and aluminum vertical bands. The instruments and switchgear are all located in the center of the dashboard to demonstrate that this is a sociable space to be in. The stereo has prime position: up top, just below the instrument pack.

The Scion brand is about personalization, and recognizes that freedom to mix and match your car is appealing to a fashion-conscious buyer who wants to do things his or her own way. How long before this ethos is exported to Europe too?

# Scion xB

| | |
|---|---|
| Design | Toyota Design |
| Engine | 1.5 in-line 4 |
| Power | 81 kW (108 bhp) @ 6000 rpm |
| Torque | 142 Nm (105 lb. ft) @ 4200 rpm |
| Gearbox | 5-speed manual |
| Installation | Front-engined/front-wheel drive |
| Front suspension | MacPherson strut |
| Rear suspension | Torsion beam |
| Brakes front/rear | Discs/drums, ABS |
| Front tires | 185/60R15 |
| Rear tires | 185/60R15 |
| Length | 3945 mm (155.3 in.) |
| Width | 1689 mm (66.5 in.) |
| Height | 1641 mm (64.6 in.) |
| Wheelbase | 2499 mm (98.4 in.) |
| Track front/rear | 1455/1430 mm (57.3/56.3 in.) |
| Curb weight | 1100 kg (2425 lb.) |

The xB model from the new Scion brand, invented by Toyota, is largely based on the Ist, which is sold in Japan. The Scion xB is also the production version of the bbX concept, which made its debut at the New York Auto Show in 2002. The xB shares its engine and transmission combinations with the xA, and is a subcompact two-box car with a clean, modern design.

The xA doesn't even try to replicate other cars. It's clearly making a statement about its functionality and simplicity, and so it stands out, which, as it happens, is what fashion-conscious buyers want. It may have been designed with a set square, but the uncompromising outline packs a lot of space inside. There is plenty of headroom, plus storage space if you choose to fold down the seats. The interior is modern, with the ubiquitous dark-gray trim and aluminum highlights, similar to the xA. The center stack houses the audio and ventilation controls, while the speedometer and odometer are offset for easier readability.

Music is central to the interior. Scion claims drivers can choose between three settings: SSP Neutral setting keeps the music in the background; SSP Hear enhances the sound with crisp highs and lows; and SSP Feel has a sound curve that lets passengers not only hear the music but feel it too.

Scion has also developed some forty accessories, ranging from fog lights, rear spoilers, and interior mats to two-tone leather-wrapped steering wheels, strut tie-bar braces, and auxiliary interior-lighting kits. The Scion models are on sale in California from the middle of 2003. In February 2004, the US market will expand to cover the south, southeast, and east coast, and a few months later Scion will complete its national rollout and launch a third product line.

# Seat Cordoba

| Engine | 1.9 in-line 4 turbo-diesel (1.2 and 1.4 in-line 4 gasoline versions also offered) |
|---|---|
| Power | 96 kW (129 bhp) @ 4000 rpm |
| Torque | 310 Nm (228 lb. ft) @ 1900 rpm |
| Gearbox | 6-speed manual |
| Installation | Front-engined/front-wheel drive |
| Front suspension | MacPherson strut |
| Brakes front/rear | Discs/discs |
| Front tires | 195/55R15 |
| Rear tires | 195/55R15 |
| Length | 4280 mm (168.5 in.) |
| Width | 1698 mm (66.9 in.) |
| Height | 1441 mm (56.7 in.) |
| Wheelbase | 2460 mm (96.9 in.) |
| 0–100 km/h (62 mph) | 9.7 sec |
| Top speed | 209 km/h (130 mph) |
| Fuel consumption | 5.1 ltr/100 km (46.1 mpg) |

The Volkswagen Group has been saying for several years that Seat must compete against Alfa Romeo in terms of design, so it launched its brand slogan "SEAT—auto emotion" to help achieve that goal.

Seat's stock rating has also been enhanced by the sporting association of entering the old Cordoba in the 1999 and 2000 world rally championships. So what will the new model accomplish?

First, the bald fact: the new Cordoba, like the car it replaces, is essentially a Seat Ibiza with a trunk instead of a hatchback; and, like all Seats, the base car is a Volkswagen, in this case the Polo, reskinned and given a new interior. Designed at Martorell, near Barcelona, the new Cordoba is, however, a rather more "emotional"-looking car, much more characterful and a little bigger than the model it replaces, which gives increased legroom and luggage capacity.

The front has a stylized hood that dips at the rounded grille, leaving raised eyebrows that rise over the headlights and lead on to the flared wheel arches. In fact, both the Cordoba and the closely related Ibiza take many styling cues from the Salsa concept unveiled at the 2000 Geneva International Motor Show. That means the Cordoba has many more curves than would have been allowed on the more austerely Teutonic Polo.

With a higher and more pronounced wedge profile, the new Cordoba has a sportier stance. At the rear, it is the new lights that really differentiate it from any Volkswagen. This is an example of how minor changes can give a standardized design its own identity—an area in which VW is increasingly cunning.

# Sivax Streetster Kira

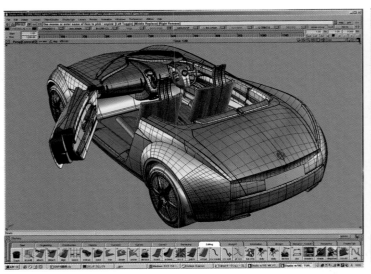
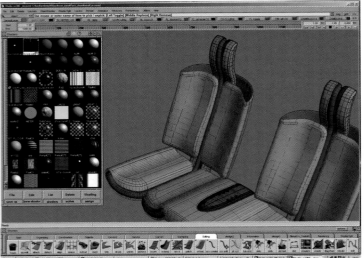

| Engine | 2.0 |
|---|---|
| Length | 3980 mm (156.7 in.) |
| Width | 1800 mm (70.9 in.) |
| Height | 1050 mm (41.3 in.) |
| Wheelbase | 2500 mm (98.4 in.) |

Sivax, a Japan-based automotive consultancy, brings us this new concept car as a technology and styling demonstrator, taking its inspiration from Tokyo's cosmopolitan street culture and fashion. The name "Kira" appears in classic Japanese literature and refers to twilled white or plain-colored silk used for elegant clothing, although it is not clear how this relates to either the exterior or the interior design.

The Kira's design is based on two intertwined wedges, one facing forward and one rearward, which meet with intersecting surfaces at the top of the doors. This creates a wedge-shaped feature running in both directions along the side of the car, removing some of the outright sports look that would otherwise be achieved by such an uncompromising open-top sports car.

At the front, the striking headlights form part of the V-shaped feature that runs alongside the hood and up to form the waistline wedge. A centerline spine, more familiar from Renault designs, rises up over the hood and splits the windshield, which is apparently modeled on a pair of sports sunglasses.

The two-plus-two interior combines leather, fabric, and metal; the instrument panel uses brass, while the floor has pearskin-finished aluminum, the product of a street-fashion design technique.

The Streetster Kira is purely a concept intended to draw attention to the development capabilities of Sivax. Although not likely to win any design awards, it has a few interesting features, particularly inside, where there is some original thought.

# Subaru B11S Coupé

The Subaru B11S Coupé is what the company calls a "Gran Utility Turismo" concept. So what's that? Historically, the manufacturer explains, this is something that combines sporty driving with comfort, functionality, and elegance.

In 2002, Kiyoshi Sugimoto was promoted to head Subaru's Product Planning and Design Department —the first time a car designer had been appointed to executive-officer level at Subaru. This signifies a new focus on drastically improving design, in the wake of the firm's decision to alter its Impreza in response to strong customer resistance.

The B11S Coupé is the first concept car designed under Sugimoto's leadership, but he was also helped by Barcelona-based and Subaru-owned Fuore Design International.

At the front, the bumper has a large gaping hole, perhaps conjuring up thoughts of a small jet plane. There are two pairs of side doors, which open gate-style and latch in the middle without a conventional B-pillar, an arrangement that, according to Subaru, allows better access to the back seats. To provide soft light inside, there is a frosted-glass roof, its design said by the company to have been inspired by traditional Japanese umbrellas.

In sharp contrast to the completely uninspiring pearl-white body color, Subaru has gone for blue for the interior, influenced by its own characteristic rally-livery color, together with extensive use of the inevitable aluminum.

Subaru's robustness, excellent technology, and success in motorsport would, in the hands of any other company, have translated into astonishing sales, but mass appeal has consistently eluded the make, and some critics have laid the blame squarely on unappealing design. We are led to expect great new things from Subaru soon; the B11S Coupé is not one of them.

| Design | Kiyoshi Sugimoto and Fuore Design International |
|---|---|
| Power | 294 kW (394 bhp) |
| Torque | 550 Nm (405 lb. ft) |
| Gearbox | 5-speed automatic |
| Installation | Front-engined/all-wheel drive |

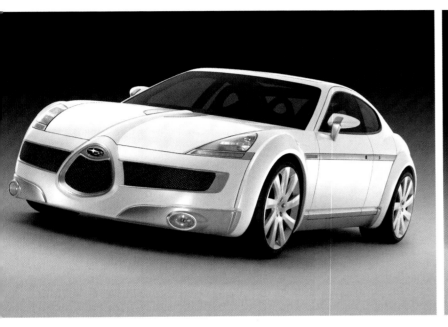

# Suzuki Forenza

| | |
|---|---|
| Design | Pininfarina |
| Engine | 2.0 in-line 4 |
| Power | 89 kW (119 bhp) @ 5400 rpm |
| Torque | 174 Nm (128 lb. ft) @ 4000 rpm |
| Gearbox | 5-speed manual |
| Installation | Front-engined/front-wheel drive |
| Front suspension | MacPherson strut |
| Rear suspension | Dual link |
| Brakes front/rear | Discs/discs |
| Front tires | P195/55R15 |
| Rear tires | P195/55R15 |
| Length | 4500 mm (177.2 in.) |
| Width | 1725 mm (67.9 in.) |
| Height | 1445 mm (56.9 in.) |
| Wheelbase | 2600 mm (102.4 in.) |
| Track front/rear | 1480/1480 mm (58.3/58.3 in.) |
| Curb weight | 1225 kg (2701 lb.) |

The American Suzuki Motor Corporation has launched its new Forenza, an affordable premium compact car created to boost Suzuki's share of the US market. Designed in Turin by Pininfarina, it is priced at a level intended to hammer the Toyota Corolla, Honda Civic, and Nissan Sentra.

The cold, commercial fact, though, is that this is being achieved thanks to GM Daewoo's cheap South Korean labor rates. Suzuki now holds a 15% stake in the fledgling GM Daewoo, and the Forenza is little more than the new Daewoo Nubira with a Japanese alias.

At the front, the small Suzuki grille sets up the lines that run over the hood to the base of the windshield. Dual sculpted cylindrical headlights initiate a waistline wedge that extends the full length of the car to the rear lights. The daylight opening line is quite low, emphasizing practicality over sportiness. The roof extends a good way rearward, giving more interior space but limiting the size of the trunk. The large tail lights, with flower-shaped beam reflectors, are similar in size to the headlights and so are an especially strong feature.

Inside is an uncluttered space that uses horizontal lines to distinguish different materials and colors on the dashboard and door trim panels. Metallic silver accents are used on the doors, instrument panels, center console, and dashboard to project a sophisticated image. The upper surface of the dashboard is designed in the form of a gentle wave with a sculpted edge that is echoed in its exterior. The instrument clusters are rimmed with metallic silver accents and, when illuminated, emit a jade-green glow that, according to Suzuki, enhances visibility during night driving. Either that or they just look pretty and help to achieve the Japanese nirvana of "customer delight."

The Forenza has a strong European design flavor, so it will be fascinating to see whether the American market buys into this vision of a "premium model" in preference to what is almost exclusively Japanese—and pretty bland—competition.

# Suzuki Verona

| | |
|---|---|
| Design | Italdesign |
| Engine | 2.5 in-line 6 |
| Power | 116 kW (155 bhp) @ 5800 rpm |
| Torque | 240 Nm (177 lb. ft) @ 4000 rpm |
| Gearbox | 4-speed automatic |
| Installation | Front-engined/front-wheel drive |
| Front suspension | MacPherson strut |
| Rear suspension | Multi-link |
| Brakes front/rear | Discs/discs |
| Front tires | P205/65R15 |
| Rear tires | P205/65R15 |
| Length | 4770 mm (187.8 in.) |
| Width | 1816 mm (71.5 in.) |
| Height | 1440 mm (56.7 in.) |
| Wheelbase | 2700 mm (106.3 in.) |
| Track front/rear | 1550/1524 mm (61/60 in.) |
| Curb weight | 1500 kg (3307 lb.) |

The new Verona is a midsized saloon designed by Italdesign in Turin. It's no coincidence that both the Forenza and the Verona have Italian names, as the former was also designed in Turin, at Pininfarina. Suzuki is banking on an injection of Mediterranean flair as the tonic the make needs to increase desirability in both the mainstream segments for which these cars are intended.

With its new and distinctly Italian design language, the Verona is intended to compete strongly against less emotional Japanese offerings in the form of the Toyota Camry, Honda Accord, and Nissan Altima. Only time will tell how that strategy works and whether Italy "sells."

The Verona is a classic three-box sedan with an aerodynamic side profile. The wide grille and large headlights reinforce its place in the middle of the pecking order of models. Fog lights embedded into the lower bumper straddle the large air intake, visually lightening the front end. The hood rises at the edges and has gentle creases that work backward toward the corners.

Italdesign's nuances are especially evident in the application of light and shade along the body side. The feature line running from the headlights through the door handles gently flares above the front and rear wheel arches, both to lengthen the car and to add visual appeal. Resting just above the flared wheel arches, it called for great ability in the designers to get the balance of proportion and effect absolutely right. The Italians are absolute masters of skills like this, and prove it brilliantly here.

Side accents include chrome door handles and color-keyed door moldings and sills, which make the body side look stronger than the lightweight and nimble front end.

# Toyota Land Cruiser

| | |
|---|---|
| Design | Toyota Motor Corporation's ED2 studio |
| Engine | 4.6 V6 (3.0 in-line 4 diesel also offered) |
| Power | 183 kW (245 bhp) @ 5200 rpm |
| Torque | 382 Nm (282 lb. ft) @ 3200 rpm |
| Gearbox | 4-speed automatic |
| Installation | Front-engined/4-wheel drive |
| Front suspension | Double wishbone |
| Rear suspension | Independent 4-link |
| Brakes front/rear | Discs/discs, BA, ABS, EBD |
| Front tires | 265/65R17 |
| Rear tires | 265/65R17 |
| Length | 4365 mm (171.9 in.) |
| Width | 1790 mm (70.5 in.) |
| Height | 1890 mm (74.4 in.) |
| Wheelbase | 2455 mm (96.7 in.) |
| Track front/rear | 1535/1535 mm (60.4 in.) |
| Curb weight | 1750 kg (3858 lb.) |
| 0–100 km/h (62 mph) | 9.5 sec |
| Top speed | 175 km/h (108.8 mph) |

The Paris Motor Show in 2002 marked the world debut of the all-new Toyota Land Cruiser. Toyota celebrated fifty years of off-roader manufacture in 2001, a half-century since the first Land Cruiser—a light, all-purpose 4×4 for civilian and military applications—took its bow, and the company's 4×4 output has been an important cornerstone of its prosperity.

The styling of the new Land Cruiser was done in Europe at ED2, Toyota's advanced design facility on the Côte d'Azur, in the south of France. This is the first time that a Land Cruiser exterior has been designed outside Japan, and therefore a measure of Toyota's confidence in its satellite studio. At the front, much of the sense of presence comes from the tough-looking, vertically veined grille, the high hood, and the bulging body moldings that protect the car when off-road. New technology on the car includes a world first: Hill-start Assist Control, for ascending slippery slopes, and Downhill Assist Control for descending.

The new Land Cruiser retains a traditional frame chassis and separate body construction, unlike the BMW X5 and Range Rover, which now have highly reinforced monocoques to take the suspension loads and provide increased stiffness. They handle almost like sedans, but a monocoque has been rejected by Toyota: not for nothing do Toyota 4×4s abound in the background of news reports from the world's most inhospitable corners; the X5 is nowhere to be seen. For the Land Cruiser is aimed at the premium luxury car segment but at the same time offers unstoppable off-road capability.

Inside, in an attempt to be both luxurious and rugged, a dull, outdated, and predominantly plastic interior has been ham-fistedly jazzed up with leather, wood, and heavy aluminum details. Too many materials in an uninspiring overall design: quite a contrast to the sophistication of the Porsche Cayenne (see p. 198) or the Volkswagen Touareg (see p. 238).

# Toyota Sienna

| Design | CALTY Design Studio |
|---|---|
| Engine | V6 |
| Power | 172 kW (230 bhp) @ 5600 rpm |
| Torque | 328 Nm (242 lb. ft) @ 3600 rpm |
| Gearbox | 5-speed automatic |
| Installation | Front-engined/all-wheel drive |
| Front suspension | MacPherson strut |
| Rear suspension | Torsion beam |
| Brakes front/rear | Discs/discs, BA, VSC (Vehicle Stability Control) |
| Front tires | 255/60R17 |
| Rear tires | 255/60R17 |
| Length | 5080 mm (200 in.) |
| Width | 1966 mm (77.4 in.) |
| Height | 1750 mm (68.9 in.) |
| Wheelbase | 3030 mm (119.3 in.) |
| Track front/rear | 1674/1709 mm (65.9/67.3 in.) |
| Curb weight | 1980 kg (4365 lb.) |
| 0–100 km/h (62 mph) | 8.6 sec |

The second-generation Sienna minivan is larger in just about every direction than its predecessor. Designed at Toyota's CALTY Design Studio in Newport Beach, California, the Sienna is an example of how minivan design can so easily look resolutely bland.

The silhouette is a mono-volume that retains a short hood and an angled rear windshield. At the front, the lights dominate the corners, while a lower grille in the bumper visually lightens it. In the hood and on the wings there are very soft feature lines that appear to break up the surfaces rather than highlighting a distinctive character. The sides use the door rubbing strips and a subtle rising feature to provide interest, while at the rear, as at the front, large lights dominate.

People buy minivans for their interiors, and the Sienna sports a two-tone design that is initiated at the center console and then rises and travels around the cabin. The control deck sits centrally, being shared visually with the front passenger, while the driver information is ahead of the steering wheel in the conventional spot.

The seating arrangement is versatile; all models have a 60/40 third-row bench seat that folds flat into the floor. With the rear seat stowed and the second-row seats removed, 244 × 122 cm (8 × 4 ft) sheets of plywood can be loaded on to the Sienna's floor. Other technical features include a DVD rear entertainment system with wireless headphones, a navigation system with rearview camera, rear seat audio, and laser cruise control.

Functional this vehicle may be, but Toyota should look to what Renault has achieved with its new Espace (see p. 202). True, the new Sienna possesses a sliding door while the Espace does not, but in every other respect the Espace is a much more compelling design.

# TVR T350

Based on the Tamora sports car, the new high-performance T350 reflects TVR's continuing involvement in motor sport. It comes with either a coupé or a targa roof and is designed to be equally at home on track and road.

With its low-slung body, relatively high waistline, dramatic curves, and bright paintwork, the whole car has the bold and brutish appearance we have come to expect from TVR. Even so, the T350 is perhaps less outlandish than the Tuscan. The uninterrupted exterior surfaces are pared down and free of the rubbing strips and other exterior ornamentation normally found on other cars. The smooth exterior and aerodynamically engineered undertrays are designed to minimize drag and maximize downforce. The front is one completely unbroken volume until the set-in doors that start the second volume—which continues through to the rear.

Inside, the leather finish is largely the same as the Tamora's, with the same analog readouts for speed and engine revs above a display that gives the driver a full range of operational information, from engine water and oil temperature, outside air temperature, and battery volts to maximum and minimum values achieved (including maximum speed).

In addition, the T350 claims some practicalities: it has a side-opening hatchback above the luggage area for easy access to a reasonably sized storage area. This feature is rather like that of the first Jaguar E-type coupé.

TVRs have never been as successfully designed as many other, more mainstream, sports cars. They use a surface language that does not totally satisfy the expectations of beauty and performance. Where a TVR comes out fighting, however, is in offering maximum performance for the money—something at which the Blackpool-based company has proved matchless.

# Volkswagen L1

| Design | Hartmut Warkuss |
|---|---|
| Engine | 0.3 1-cylinder diesel |
| Power | 6.3 kW (8.5 bhp) @ 4000 rpm |
| Gearbox | 6-speed automatic |
| Installation | Mid-engined/rear-wheel drive |
| Front suspension | Double wishbone |
| Rear suspension | De Dion |
| Length | 3470 mm (136.6 in.) |
| Width | 1250 mm (49.2 in.) |
| Curb weight | 290 kg (639 lb.) |
| Top speed | 120 km/h (75 mph) |
| Fuel consumption | 0.99 ltr/100 km (237.6 mpg) |

Volkswagen's outgoing chairman, Dr Ferdinand Piech, handed over control of the VW group to Bernd Pischetsreider in 2002. He drove to the company's annual general meeting in Hamburg in a real-life demonstration of the L1, a small, lightweight concept car that gives exceptional fuel economy of just 0.99 liters of diesel per 100 km (237.6 mpg).

Such amazing thrift is possible because the car is technology-driven in every respect. The conceptual necessity for a small frontal area led to an unusually narrow and very flat body form. The body was developed in a wind tunnel and is made completely of carbon-fiber composites. An example of the lengths to which VW has gone to save weight is that the shell isn't even painted but simply laid bare and tensioned over the magnesium spaceframe.

The tandem seating arrangement is critical to the small frontal area, the occupants getting in and out through a single gullwing door. Inside, the seat frames are made of magnesium and covered with firm fabric instead of the more usual padded upholstery.

Volkswagen claims the L1 isn't merely a research vehicle but also a high-tech special vehicle that incorporates numerous practical and convenient features. For example, there is a stowage compartment of 0.08 cubic meters (2.8 cubic ft) at the rear, a reversing camera that helps when maneuvering, automatic locking and unlocking of the gullwing door, and a starter button in the cockpit that allows keyless operation.

The cost of the materials alone would make the L1 a totally unfeasible proposition for production. Even so, it's an intriguing demonstration of what efficiencies can be achieved when cost is no object.

# Volkswagen Touareg

| Design | Hartmut Warkuss |
|---|---|
| Engine | 5.0 V10 TDi (3.2 V6 gasoline, 4.2 V8 gasoline, and 2.5 in-line 5 TDi also offered) |
| Power | 230 kW (313 bhp) @ 3750 rpm |
| Torque | 750 Nm (553 lb. ft) @ 2000 rpm |
| Gearbox | 6-speed automatic |
| Installation | Front-engined/4-wheel drive |
| Front suspension | Double wishbone |
| Rear suspension | Double wishbone |
| Brakes front/rear | Discs/discs, ABS, EBD, ESP, ASR |
| Front tires | 255/55R18 |
| Rear tires | 255/55R18 |
| Length | 4754 mm (187.2 in.) |
| Width | 1928 mm (75.9 in.) |
| Height | 1703 mm (67 in.) |
| Wheelbase | 2855 mm (112.4 in.) |
| 0–100 km/h (62 mph) | 7.8 sec |
| Top speed | 225 km/h (140 mph) |
| Fuel consumption | 12.2 ltr/100 km (19.3 mpg) |

The first off-road vehicle from Volkswagen, if you discount the obscure and militaristic Iltis of the late 1970s, the Touareg is long awaited and comes at a time of strong competition from Volvo's XC-90, BMW's X5, Nissan's Murano, and the Porsche Cayenne—with which it shares its platform and entire basic structure.

Volkswagen seems to be reacting to the criticism raised about unclear product differentiation between its Skoda, Seat, and Volkswagen brands—by moving Volkswagen upmarket. This is the second recent car confirming this theory, after Volkswagen recently launched the Phaeton luxury sedan.

The Touareg is a luxury off-roader sitting at the high end of the SUV market. Like the rest of the VW range, it uses tight, solid-looking surfaces to project strength and quality. At the front, the grille has chrome detailing, and there are extra air intakes in the bumper to break up the increased height and try to stop it resembling a Passat on steroids.

The rear is satisfyingly finished, with bold taillights, a drooping rear-glass line, and an aluminum underguard complete with twin exhaust pipes that hint at the Touareg's mud-defying capability. The styling is clearly, and cleverly, aimed at both European and North American markets.

Technology inside the Touareg includes independent climate control for four passengers, and a keyless-access system whereby the car recognizes its driver via the key transponder in his pocket and releases the door when he touches the handle. Pushing a button then starts the car. The interior design has a two-tone dashboard and mixes leather with dark-wood details for a luxurious feel.

A well-executed and probably surefire hit, barring any snags when buyers actually take delivery.

# Volvo VCC

| | |
|---|---|
| Design | José Diaz de la Vega |
| Engine | 2.6 in-line 6 turbo |
| Power | 186 kW (250 bhp) |
| Gearbox | Auto shift manual |
| Installation | Front-engined/all-wheel drive |
| Front tires | 245/40R20 |
| Rear tires | 245/40R20 |
| Length | 4915 mm (193.5 in.) |
| Height | 1439 mm (56.7 in.) |
| Wheelbase | 3095 mm (121.9 in.) |
| Track front/rear | 1612/1630 mm (63.5/64.2 in.) |
| Curb weight | 1300 kg (2866 lb.) |
| Fuel consumption | 6.5 ltr/100 km (36.2 mpg) |

Volvo's "Versatility Concept Car" is a resolutely Swedish vision of how such a format might be reflected in a future product of the Ford-owned make.

The VCC has a number of typical Volvo design elements. Its broad shoulders, for example, are even more accentuated than those of the already bulging Volvo V70 and S80. The V shape of the hood starts with the grille and develops into the "Volvo bridge" along the cant rail.

For inspiration, Volvo's designers have drawn heavily on the firm's design heritage. The distinctive rear design, with a deep glass tailgate, was also featured in the Safety Concept Car of 2001 and can trace its roots to the 1971 Volvo 1800ES. The large, distinguished grille is descended from the 1968 Volvo 164.

The VCC offers a number of technological innovations. At the front there are slim, vertically stacked headlights; one of the two lights uses a system known as "Static Bending Light," with three light units aimed at different angles. The topmost unit points straight ahead and acts as a conventional dipped beam. As the car turns to one side or the other, sensors linked to the steering activate units two and three to illuminate the direction in which the car is turning, massively enhancing safety at night.

The interior has a minimal number of visible design features. There is a "floating" center console finished in anodized aluminum, and beneath the load floor are two useful storage compartments, one heated and one chilled. The roof has a solar panel that provides power for the ambient-air-cleaning system, which continuously cleans the air inside the car even when the engine is not running.

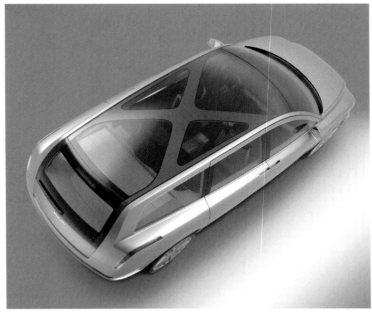

The Design Process

Profiles of Key Designers

# The Design Process

In this section we showcase three leading automotive designers who have made an outstanding contribution to the industry. Chris Bangle of BMW, Patrick le Quément of Renault, and J. Mays of Ford have been chosen for their renowned ability to reshape the design language of the makes with which they are associated. As a result of this exceptional skill, each has risen to a very senior position within his company.

Designing any car is a challenging and intricate process, and the final design comes at the end of a long road. From the earliest stages and all along the way, pure design is complemented by other disciplines, particularly marketing, engineering, and manufacturing, all of which play an important role. Nowadays, car designers have to meet so many legal requirements that a specific function called "engineering feasibility" exists to play a critical role in ensuring their ideas conform to the regulations. Among the features considered during this process are forward and rearward vision, wheel-arch coverage, ground clearance, seatbelt mounting points, bumper impact zones, and vehicle width.

At a more strategic level, design achievements are determined by the importance the company's main board attaches to design. The directors determine both the resources allocated to design and how much influence design will have on the product planning strategy. Internal politics often affects the final result, so that, while all carmakers claim design is important, not all treat it accordingly.

Companies such as Fiat and Renault in Europe and Chrysler in the USA are particularly design-led, and many others value design to varying degrees. In adopting this approach, they are hoping that their cars will stand out from the rest and attract potential buyers' attention. By contrast, most Japanese car manufacturers prefer design to be led by market research, which explains their tendency to produce very practical and, by comparison with other markets, less flamboyant designs. This is no bad thing, for everyone knows the great successes the Japanese have had in creating high-quality cars that are sold in their millions to people who look for nothing more demanding than total reliability and comfort. Even cars with the most uninspired design work perfectly.

**Above from top**
A sketch of a Volvo

A rendering of a Cadillac

Its detail is rarely seen by the public, but there is a progression between concept and production launches that results in the concept car being toned down significantly to appeal to a more conservative public. Most people need their cars for practical purposes and wouldn't risk being ridiculed for spending their money on something weird. Concepts grab media coverage for their exciting designs and innovative solutions, but the final production model is usually tailored to capture the most sales at the least cost. Happily, a few cars, including the Audi TT, Chrysler Crossfire, Ford Ka, and Nissan Z, don't lose too much of their original appeal in the process.

All major car companies are well aware of the importance of product positioning for their models and those of their competitors. The market is divided into various vehicle segments, with cars of similar length and width grouped for purposes of comparison. Manufacturers aim to keep a clear view of the segment in which a proposed vehicle belongs as that segment evolves.

A further consideration is that, throughout the world, socioeconomic, demographic, and political

changes all have a direct influence in shaping emerging markets for new cars. The car manufacturer attempts to predict these movements, so as to be ready to exploit gaps in the market as they appear. Market research then helps to formulate a high-level spec for a new vehicle, which designers work from and product planners refer to when considering the manufacturing and platform strategies. Recent successes in identifying new segments include retro-inspired designs, such as the new Mini and the Chrysler PT Cruiser, the rapid expansion of the SUV market, and the MCC Smart city car.

When market research and product positioning analysis are complete, work begins on identifying the engine and suspension concept needed to deliver the performance required, along with the appropriate occupant and luggage space. This information is used to create a drawing of the "vehicle package," which is given to the designers so that they have "hard points" from which to work.

In the design studio, sketching will have begun on the vehicle's overall shape and specific features before colored renderings are made of the exterior and interior. These activities happen alongside engineering design, to help reduce product development times.

Ideas for the exterior and interior may take the form of an evolution of previous models, as with the Jaguar XJ, or they might try to broach radically new territory, as with the Porsche Cayenne. Hundreds of ideas are explored over, typically, three months, with a small selection being digitally constructed for transferal—via milling machines—to 40% scale models made of clay. A selection process then establishes the preferred scale models, and these are worked up into much more refined and detailed full-sized clay models. It often takes a year to progress from initial sketch to final approval of the exterior model; the more complex and detailed interior usually follows some six months later.

Traditionally, the interior has followed the form of the exterior, with the chosen outer shape and proportions directly affecting what can be achieved inside the car. Yet in the future we may see this "outside-in" design priority challenged, as companies are investing more in, and becoming much more imaginative about, interior design.

**Opposite top**
A clay scale model is created

**Opposite bottom**
Milling a full-sized clay model

**Above**
Refinement of a clay model of the Jaguar X-Type

# Chris Bangle

Unlikely as it may seem for the man in charge of BMW's design destiny today, Christopher Edward Bangle was born at Ravenna, Ohio. Four years later, in 1960, his family moved to Wausau, Wisconsin, and this is where Chris grew up. Bangle's career direction was by no means set at an early stage. In 1975 he began studying philosophy, literature, history, and psychology with the intention of becoming a Methodist minister. However, after deciding this wasn't the direction for him, he applied to the Art Center College of Design, in Pasadena, California, showing a portfolio of his own designs for items as diverse as sewing machines, telephones, cars, and comic strips. Accepted for the Transdesign program in 1977, he moved to California. During summer vacation he would return to Wausau, where he worked designing machines and tools for Hartkopf Associates, an industrial-design studio run by Jerry Hartkopf, one of the designers of the Chicago School.

After graduating from Pasadena in 1981, Bangle was offered a job at Opel in Germany, where he began his career as a car designer. Initially he worked on interiors under Kurt Ludvig, who led the team on the Tech 1 show car, and then he moved on to the Corsa Spider and Junior. Presented at the Frankfurt Motor Show in 1983, the Opel Junior won first prize in the 1984 Car Design Awards. Bangle also worked on the dashboards and cabins of the Vectra and Senator production models. After only two years at Opel, Bangle became assistant chief designer at this German outpost of General Motors, a position he held for two more years before joining Fiat in Turin in 1984.

In 1985, Bangle's area of work changed to exterior design at the Fiat Design Center. He was chosen for this task specifically because of his experience in interior design: the intention was that he should apply his thinking to exteriors. In looking at exterior design from the user's viewpoint, he designed cars from the inside out. At Opel, the design process had been mostly two-dimensional: dozens of sketches were made, which were eventually worked up into 3D models. In contrast, at Fiat, designers worked in model form as early as possible in the process, and a large team of modelers was on hand to produce scale plaster models by the hundred.

**Above**
Chris Bangle

**Opposite, clockwise from top left**
BMW 3 Series
BMW X5
BMW Z3
BMW Z3 Coupé

It was in Turin, says Bangle, that he learned to think three-dimensionally. Fiat had no established house style and designers were encouraged to think freely and approach car design from all directions. Nevertheless, Bangle's team was frustrated, and most of the time overshadowed, because Fiat's management chose to outsource many projects to Bertone, Pininfarina, and Italdesign. Competition with these outside consultancies—despite their impressive repertoires and the high esteem in which they were consequently held—often left Bangle disaffected. He came to see his role within Fiat as to provide an in-house creative benchmark that the favored design agency could be measured against.

Eventually, Bangle was given a free hand to design two products; the spectacular results were the 1993 Fiat Coupé and the Alfa Romeo 145 of 1994. By 1992, he was head of the Fiat Design Center, but it was at this point that he was offered the opportunity to become director of the BMW Design Center in Munich. It wasn't a decision he dawdled over.

Bangle was the first head of design at BMW to have formal training in automotive design. Wolfgang Reitzle, then in charge at BMW, hired him for his European experience and his knowledge of how design fits into corporate culture. At BMW, Bangle has been responsible for the entire current range of conservative "number series" cars, which have enjoyed continually growing success around the world. More innovative Bangle-inspired designs that have brought new market share and visibility to BMW include the Z3 roadster, the retro Z8 roadster, the hugely successful X5, and the new Z4 roadster. Another evolution is that the 3-series coupé now shares less exterior structure with its sedan counterparts, which gives it its own sports identity.

Other, more recent concept-car projects led by Bangle include the Z9, which explores possible future design ideas for BMW, and the CS1 concept, which recently evolved into the Z4 roadster. Under Bangle's leadership, BMW bought the Californian Designworks/USA business, which had previously acted as a consultant to the company, and gained exclusive access to the "freethinking" Californian culture fostered by Adrian van Hooydonk, a Dutch designer who also studied at the Art Center College of Design.

**Above**
BMW Z8

**Opposite top**
BMW Z9 concept

**Opposite bottom**
BMW CS1 concept

One of the most dramatic recent changes in BMW design has been the use of "flame surfacing" —the term invented by Bangle to describe the combination of convex and concave surfaces. Flame surfacing caused much interest among the design community on the CS1 concept and the earlier X Coupé, an asymmetrical coupé with one door longer than the other (a feature last seen in 1975's ill-starred AMC Pacer).

We can expect BMW, as it seeks to capture new market share, to launch more innovative new products that transcend the boundaries of its current models. These will include new sports cars, crossover vehicles, and SUVs. Recent examples are the xActivity concept and the still-unrevealed replacement for the X5.

# J. Mays

J. Mays became Vice President of Design at the Ford Motor Company in October 1997. His massive global responsibilities now include shaping the design direction of not just Ford but also Mazda, Mercury, Lincoln, Volvo, Jaguar, Land Rover, and Aston Martin.

Since taking up this role, Mays (who keeps his first name to himself) has completed the development of several new production models, including the Ford GT40, the 2002 Ford Thunderbird, the 2002 Ford Explorer, and the Mercury Mountaineer. He has led the development of several concept cars, including the Ford Forty-Nine, the Jaguar F-type, and the Volvo Safety Car, and he has played an instrumental role in the redesign of the Ford Motor Company's auto-show display stands.

Born in 1954 in Pauls Valley, Oklahoma, Mays is married with one son. He graduated in 1980 from the Art Center College of Design, in Pasadena, California, where he studied automotive design, and began his career in Ingolstadt, Germany, as an exterior designer for Audi. Here he was recognized for the exterior treatment of the aerodynamic third-generation Audi 80.

Mays remained in Germany throughout the early part of his career. By 1983 he was working for BMW in Munich, developing exterior designs for the BMW 5 and 8 Series cars, but the following year he returned to Audi as senior designer. Here he developed aerodynamic research vehicles for the Audi Rally/TransAm programs and full-scale model proposals for the Audi 100, Volkswagen Golf and Polo, and Audi Cabrio. He also worked on the Avus, Audi's first concept car constructed of aluminum, which featured a twelve-cylinder engine.

He left Europe in 1989 and returned to the USA to work as chief designer for Volkswagen America's Design Center in Simi Valley, California. His main achievement was to establish an infrastructure for the development of full-scale models, but he was also responsible for the design and branding of the Volkswagen Concept One, the precursor of the New Beetle.

In 1993, Mays returned to Germany to work for Audi as design director responsible for worldwide design development strategy. Ever restless, he left the company two years later to become Vice

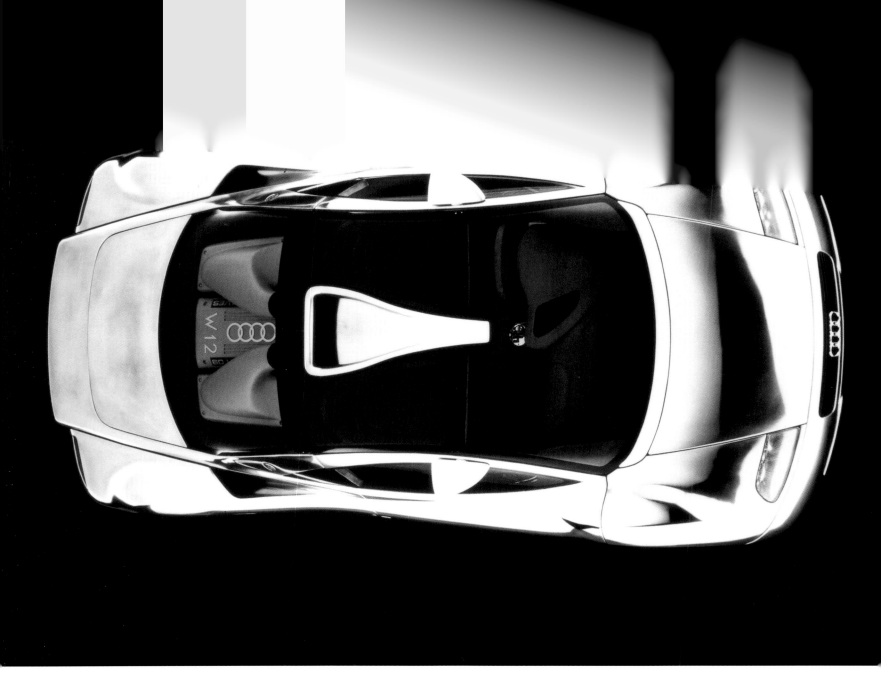

**Opposite**
J. Mays

**Above**
Audi Avus concept

President for Design Development at SHR Perceptual Management in Scottsdale, Arizona, and stayed there from 1995 to 1997.

But cars are Mays's love and, now that he is holding down his monumental job at Ford, one indulgence is building a team to design the new Ford GT40, which echoes the 1960s racer and is intended as a rolling celebration of Ford's centenary in 2003. Other concept cars designed by Mays's team include a sleek black model, inspired by 1940s models, named the Forty-Nine. Mays has moved beyond designing within conventional fashions, preferring to create new car fashions and influence new niche markets. He tells his designers not to follow trends but instead to be somewhat anti-fashion. His view is that contemporary fashionable design will never be as highly regarded as design that is timeless.

Other fields of design, especially architecture, have influenced Mays, with the result that much of his work uses clean, taut surfaces, mostly free of unnecessary features. The years he spent in Germany working for Audi, together with his time in California, have immersed him in the modern design clearly seen in Ford products today.

Mays has received numerous professional awards and accolades. In February 2002, he received Harvard Design School's annual Excellence in Design Award, given to individuals whose creative endeavors have made a significant contribution to society that affects everyday lives. In September of that year, he was presented with the Don Kubly Professional Attainment Award of the Art Center College of Design. His design career was also the subject of *Retrofuturism: The Car Design of J. Mays*, an exhibition held in Los Angeles at Geffen Contemporary, part of the Museum of Contemporary Art, in November 2002. According to Mays, "Retrofuturism" means the design of a futuristic vehicle inspired by the mindset of a particular culture. A prime example of Retrofuturism, derived from a 1950s mindset, is the Thunderbird; another, from a 1960s one, the Ford GT40.

**Above**
Volkswagen Concept1 (which became the new Beetle)

**Opposite top**
BMW 850i

**Opposite bottom**
BMW 5 Series

# Patrick le Quément

Patrick le Quément is one of the most talented and highly respected designers in the business. Born in Marseilles in 1945, he spent his early years in France, but following his father's death his mother sent him to a boarding school in England. At St Augustine Abbey College, in Ramsgate, Kent, he not only eventually mastered the English language but also became a prefect.

After school, Le Quément decided to stay in England, graduating from the Birmingham Institute of Art and Design in 1966 with a degree in product design. He then began his career as an automotive designer at Simca's styling department in Paris. After a year at Simca, working mainly on interiors, he struck out on his own, setting up the Style International product-design agency with fellow designer John Pinko. Only a year later, there were nationwide strikes in France and the business suffered. In 1968, Le Quément was taken on by Ford, where he remained for seventeen years, moving up through the design ranks in the UK, Germany, the USA, Brazil, Australia, and Japan until, at thirty-six, he became the company's youngest-ever Design Director.

In 1985, he moved to Volkswagen and founded the Strategic and Advanced Design Center. He says his greatest achievement there was to convince the board that the recently acquired SEAT should retain and build on Spanish influences and not become solely a production facility for Volkswagen models. Le Quément had been at VW for two years when the chairman of Renault, Louis Schweitzer, asked him to take over as head of the design department. From the start of his leadership, Renault's design progressed exponentially, and the company is now producing work that is well ahead of its time.

Schweitzer told Le Quément that his task was to come up with strong concepts whenever possible, and with a distinctive style in all cases. Renault Design is based at the Renault Technocenter on the outskirts of Paris. An unusual feature of the company is that Corporate Design reports directly to Schweitzer's office, testimony to the overwhelming importance the chairman attributes to design.

Under Le Quément's leadership, a number of models have entered automotive history: the Twingo in 1992, the Scénic in 1996, the Kangoo in 1997, and, more recently, the new Renault luxury-car range, with

**Above**
Patrick le Quément

**Opposite top**
Renault Argos concept

**Opposite bottom**
Renault Initiale concept

the Avantime as its flagship in 2001, the Vel Satis launched in 2002, and the new Espace IV. The new Mégane II has also brought Renault's daring styling to the more traditional mid-range segment.

Le Quément's strategy has, in the main, worked wonders for Renault sales, particularly of small and family cars. However, a blow to his bold design ethos was delivered by the company's sudden decision in 2003 to axe the highly innovative Avantime after fewer than five thousand had been sold. It seems, perversely, that progressive design is fine in the mass market but stumbles in the cautious and deeply conservative executive-car sector.

Over the past decade. a number of Renault concept cars, both testbeds for new ideas and showcases for the latest trends, have also imprinted themselves on people's minds. The Argos sports car from 1994, for example, with its pure and simple lines, brought a breath of fresh air to automotive design. The strong Initiale, in 1995, and the Vel Satis concept, in 1998, also helped to launch the new visual identity of the brand by presenting these top-of-the-range models. The "Touch Design" concept, an approach to interior controls intended to make them more recognizable to the user, was unveiled on the Talisman concept in 2001, and has now been launched in production on the Mégane II. The pretty Ellypse concept featured in this book (see p. 200) reveals a new way of designing cars with a view to sustainable development.

The pretty Ellypse concept featured in this book (see p. 200)

At the end of 1994, Le Quément became Senior Vice President for Quality and Corporate Design. In 1999, Renault took a controlling stake in Japan's Nissan, and Schweitzer asked his trusted guru to devote his attentions once more exclusively to design, for both Renault and Nissan, to bring greater creativity to both brands as rapidly as possible. The result is that the most recent Nissan products, such as the Primera and the Micra, have a much stronger visual identity.

Among the many honors Le Quément has received are France's Grand Prix National de la Création Industrielle, in 1992, and a doctorate from the University of Central England in 1996. In 1998, France made him a Chevalier of the Ordre National de la Légion d'Honneur. For his many years of creativity at Renault he was given the Raymond Loewy Foundation's Designer Award in 2002.

**Opposite from top**
Renault Kangoo
Renault Avantime
Renault Mégane

**Above**
Renault Talisman concept

Why Concept Cars?

Concept Car Evolutions

# Why Concept Cars?

Ever since the 1930s, concept cars have been shown at exhibitions. Various pulse-raising labels have been adopted to describe these non-production models, which are visions of the future: terms like "show cars," "image cars," "dream cars," along with "concept cars" itself, are all worn smooth with overuse.

But let's call them concept cars, as it's the most accurate description. As the embodiments of evolving ideas, they are intended to prepare the way for future production models, to anticipate design trends, and, sometimes, to stake out a claim for the brand in new and uncharted product and market territory. There are also specifically "research" cars that exist first and foremost to showcase technical expertise. Both types of vehicle act as intermediaries, showing potential customers what they can expect to be able to buy in the future. This function is critical, as it ensures that a strong, pent-up demand already exists by the time the company is in a position to launch the product.

In the 1930s, during the Great Depression, car builders vied fiercely for the few sales around. The "wow" factor became one important method of attracting new customers, and so Harley Earl, head of General Motors' Styling Division, which he established in 1936, decided to create a fantasy car to test public opinion. The 1939 Y-Job was his dream machine that would evaluate popular taste. Based on a standard Buick chassis, the two-seater sports car was stretched to 6 meters (20 ft). It also boasted the never-before-seen combination of pop-up headlights, flush-fitting door handles, a horizontal grille, and an electrically operated top. Earl was a pioneer of the concept car, and his innovations also included the use of full-sized clay models for rapid evaluation and styling alterations. Another pre-war show car was a Cadillac V16 Aerodynamic Coupe, which GM exhibited at *A Century of Progress* in Chicago in 1933.

At Ford in the 1950s and 1960s, the dream cars of styling head George Walker went from just about credible to totally extreme. The X-100, for example, influenced later Thunderbird styling, while the Mystere would have been at home in a science-fiction movie, the Lincoln Futura became Batman's transport on 1960s television, and the Ford Gyron, which incorporated a huge gyroscope, was the product of a space-age imagination run wild.

In some cases today, concept cars promise slightly more than the production versions can deliver, not least in their design. The concept car is usually overly bold, in order to capture media and public attention. This is a way of assessing what the customer is likely to accept. Sometimes designers can't push design forwards as quickly as they would like, but instead have to move more slowly to allow the buying public to catch up and become used to new ideas.

The design of a concept car is rarely set in stone, so there is no guarantee that every detail that has won the heart of the showgoer will turn up in the production version. Often a specific styling feature turns out to be too impractical or expensive for the consumer market; and, of course, the car must be capable of being factory-assembled efficiently, which also sometimes demands changes to the concept design.

An all-important, if unquantifiable, factor at motor shows is public reaction to the concept. Is the reception enthusiastic or merely lukewarm? No elaborate surveys are needed: the mood at the launch stand is often a reliable starting point,

especially if key company executives are present to soak it all up. The response of the international media, too, is analysed very carefully, and at the same time market-research teams corroborate the subjective impressions obtained at the motor show.

Here are a couple of examples of the importance that concept cars and "technology demonstrators" have today. Introduced in 2001, the X Coupé was the car that heralded most explicitly the intention of design director Chris Bangle to move BMW design away from its long-established evolutionary path. It was an asymmetrical design with proportions that were not all typical of BMW. The X Coupé also introduced "flame surfacing," a radical language of exterior form that generated much concern in industry and press circles about BMW's direction. The mainly negative reaction was not surprising, given how far the aesthetic departed from contemporary norms. However, since the new BMW Z4, with its flame-surface language, was introduced this year, it has gained wide acclaim, and this is in no small part due to the fact that the new direction had already been unveiled in an "extreme" form two years earlier.

The Mercedes-Benz F400 Carving was a technology demonstrator that made a stunning debut at the Tokyo Motor Show in 2001. It was never intended to be a production car: among other apparently fanciful features, it sported gullwing doors, electronic camber adjustment, and active suspension, and it had no roof. However, much of the advanced engineering showcased on the Carving is gradually working its way into Mercedes-Benz production models. Wrapped up in such an eye-catching concept, it received massive press coverage. This was exactly what Mercedes-Benz desired as a way to trumpet its brand-new technology.

When concept cars are displayed, the public obtains a tantalizing look at the automotive future, and manufacturers get either positive feedback—which confirms product planners' hunches—or negative vibes—which prevent costly marketing mistakes. Today, shareholder confidence is vital, too. Concept cars often prove a company is aiming in the right direction, and with expectant customers just waiting for the next model to roll off the production line, that confirmation can only be good for the share price.

**Above**
The 1955 Lincoln Futura, with its domed roofs and huge, fin-like wings, became known as the "Batmobile" after being customized by George Barris to appear in the 1960s American TV series *Batman*.

**Opposite from top**
A real achievement in combining technology with fantastic design was the Ford Gyron of 1961. A huge gyroscope, the company assured everyone, kept this two-wheeler upright at all times.

An asymmetrical body with one door longer than the other may have practical benefits, but the X Coupé, which dates from 2001, is now most importantly recognized as the public launchpad for BMW's new "flame surfacing" design language.

# BMW CS1
# BMW Z4

The CS1 concept was drastically changed before being launched for real as the Z4 roadster in 2003. The original was, in simplistic terms, a small 3-Series four-seater convertible with "flame surfacing" design language. The body sides were more upright and the overall shape was much squarer than in the Z4. It's clear that the CS1 was a design exercise, as several elements were unfeasible for a production car. Probably the most glaring of these was the lack of storage space for any sort of retractable roof system; this would have taken trunk space, and that would have meant no room for luggage—unthinkable for a four-seater BMW. The keynote "flame surfaces" were also used on the interior as knee bolsters and for trim on top of the aluminum dashboard structure—unlikely to pass safety regulations. Also, the seats were thin and very sporty, whereas BMWs combine luxury with sportiness. The CS1 didn't have enough comfort to be credible as a future model.

However, the concept got excellent critical reviews at the same time as BMW decided that a more curvaceous, more emotional body style was needed for its Z3 replacement. So the CS1-derived Z4 production model was shown in 2002, at the Paris Motor Show. It's a well-resolved sports car, one far more convincingly conceived than the often derided Z3.

It's unlikely BMW would use the CS1 concept to spawn another convertible that might sit below the Z4 in the marketplace; its well-proven *modus operandi* is to chase higher profits from more expensive models. Yet the dramatic evolution of the CS1 into the Z4 demonstrates how much design activity is going on within the company—another vital element in BMW's ability to stay ahead of its rivals while making a lot of money.

# Chrysler Pacifica

Among the evolutions compared in this section, the Pacifica's has been one of the most straightforward. A core vehicle in Chrysler's product planning, the Pacifica was never a speculative concept: it was more a way to prime the perhaps sceptical buying public for the production version. Still, the concept played an important role: to whet the appetites of potential SUV buyers—and prevent them writing out checks for models made by competitors.

Only four months passed before the production version was launched, at the New York International Auto Show in 2002, with only very minor design changes. Most of the engineering had already been completed at the time of the concept's launch, but some updates sneaked in, including new rectangular headlights, and much more extensive use of black trim around the lower body; this effectively makes the car more ground-hugging, while simultaneously boosting its ruggedness. And finally, rubbing strips and chunkier handles were added to the doors.

# GM AUTOnomy
# GM Hy-wire

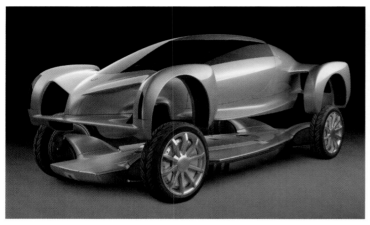 

The GM AUTOnomy captured a huge amount of media attention after its launch. Its unique "skateboard" design looked so futuristic that it didn't really connect with today's car designs at all, but it laid the path perfectly for its successor, the Hy-wire. The AUTOnomy was all about its intrinsic technology: the powertrain, fuel cells, and driving components necessary to propel it were sealed inside the skateboard. The concept was designed so that different bodies could be fixed on to the chassis, depending on the owner's needs. This is a great idea in principle, but so forward-looking was it that it seemed we shouldn't expect to see one on the roads in the next twenty years.

The Hy-wire has changed all that, however, and comes complete with a popular MPV-style body. At the same time it's a fully drivable car—even motoring journalists have been allowed behind its bizarre-shaped wheel. The Hy-wire is unique in that it's the world's first working vehicle to combine a hydrogen fuel cell with by-wire technology, including brake-by-wire, steer-by-wire, and accelerate-by-wire. GM's vision is to have affordable fuel-cell vehicles on the road by the end of this decade, so the Hy-wire, and other future cars that will evolve from the AUTOnomy, have just a few short years to gain market acceptance.

These vehicles are the best example today of the important role concept cars play in showcasing technology and building the case for a new future market, while at the same time gauging the opinion of the automotive press and public about highly futuristic models aimed at maximum market penetration.

# MG X80
# MG XPower SV

After MG Rover acquired Qvale, a budding Italian sports-car company, in 2001, it spent a year assessing the best way to create a flagship model for the MG brand from the existing Qvale Mangusta. The initial vision was for the X80 coupé and convertible. MG would take the Qvale chassis, underbody, and powertrain and then reskin the sub-structure to create a high-performance MG that would, it was hoped, compete with the Porsche Carrera.

But the business case never stacked up because the amount of changes necessary to meet the latest crash legislation and quality targets, especially for the convertible, meant the engineering cost would never have been recoverable against projected sales.

An alternative strategy was needed, and so, under the direction of Peter Stevens, the MG XPower SV emerged: a much more extreme high-performance sports car. The benefits of this are that lower sales at higher prices would make composites technology more appropriate and thus reduce tooling investment. The convertible version was also abandoned in favor of other, specially tuned, competition-oriented options for the coupé model. This will be offered in a racing form that buyers can enter in a one-make race series.

The new MG is now much more aggressive, with huge trims running completely around its lower edge, and numerous aerodynamic aids for engine cooling and counteracting downforce.

As with all such high-performance models, much of the aim is to achieve media coverage, both from the one-make race series and from the "fast car" profile, which attracts extensive coverage in the enthusiast press. But the tricky part for MG is that it desperately needs alternative affordable models that people can buy as a result of all this glamorous image-building.

# Opel Signum 2
# Opel Signum

The Opel Signum2 concept has evolved into the production Opel Signum, and now this mold-breaking executive car is on sale throughout Europe. The new Signum sits in the Opel range above the Vectra, and aims to combine the traveling environment of an upmarket sedan with the space of an MPV or estate.

The original concept has been slightly adapted and refined during the eighteen months that have elapsed between its unveiling and the production launch. There have been sundry exterior changes, the more noticeable of which are the replacement of gloss wheels by satin ones, the addition of both door rubbing strips and a black trim around the bottom of the whole car; the use of a narrower front grille to incorporate a body-colored band at its sides; and headlights that now line up with the grille and lack their former horizontal detail. At the rear, the CHMSL (centrally high-mounted stop light) is now smaller, and the rear-light lenses are red with a lower white strip.

There has been more substantial evolution inside the car—or, more accurately, a safer design has been adopted, using more traditional Opel materials and design language. Gone are the minimalist digital dashboard and the Formula 1-style steering wheel in favor of a more Germanic, darker interior. Numerous buttons and nickel-colored trim give an upmarket feel that suits the car better.

Overall, though, the Signum has maintained the essence and proportions of the concept right through to launch. This indicates that Opel has received favorable market-research reviews during the car's development—including a reality check on the interior.

# Renault Ellypse
# Renault Scénic

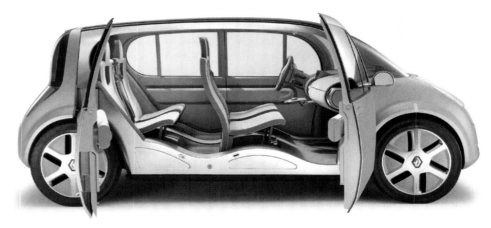

Aside from being a forerunner to the new Scénic, albeit with only a few shared similarities in the end, the Ellypse was a technology demonstrator and a research vehicle with a focus on inbuilt design friendliness. So how was it so friendly and why was that so important?

When you look at the Ellypse, you notice first the two-tone monospace and its large doors, which together create a strong, semicircular profile. The warm, blue-tinted almond front has a slightly rising graphic either side of the badge, and this profile is void of any projections, which gives the car a friendly look without making it too "cuddly."

The Ellypse's exterior proportions are kept in the new Scénic, but none of the playful door features. The new car plays it much safer. At the rear is the stepped-out trunk that typifies the Renault range today. Here the design shares the Ellypse's vision, but there has been much resculpting.

Inside, the new Scénic retains "Touch Design" controls; these are easier on the eye and continue the friendly personality of the exterior to the minimalist interior. In both the Scénic and the new Espace, "Touch Design" has been taken out of the concept environment and productionized. The Ellypse's bright interior has been dropped in favor of a calming one that is more in tune with the larger Espace model.

Other cheerful internal features include the wavy floor, which supports the seats with their innovative function that allows each seat to go from a "road" to a horizontal "rest" position by pressing a button in the front door panel.

So, in the Scénic, apart from the overall proportions, the design features of the Ellypse have been dropped in favor of a more traditional Renault—for the moment.

The Ellypse has demonstrated that Renault is seriously assessing how much people want friendly-looking cars. If they do want them, and Renault can capture this emotion and exploit it throughout its range, the French carmaker will benefit here from a unique selling point.

Certainly the Ellypse pushed Renault design forward, and, thankfully, we can expect more concepts in the future that will be equally exploratory.

# Renault Espace

Six months elapsed between the concept and production launches of the new Espace; just for once there were virtually no visible changes between the initial showing and the final offering, such is Renault's belief in the direction it has chosen for the new Espace.

In fact, the evolution from the third-generation Espace to this latest one has not been shared with the public at all, for there must have been many alternative ideas that remain buried in the vaults of the Paris studio. Instead, Renault has chosen to wait until the final version is ready before whetting the appetite of potential customers—no doubt to squeeze maximum sales from the outgoing model.

The outgoing Espace was extremely successful, even with greatly intensified competition from other makes, but the latest model exudes a renewed focus on interior comfort and flexibility that leaves rivals trailing once more.

The fourth-generation Espace has been made more like a sedan, with individual belt-in seats mounted on floor rails to allow virtually any seating configuration. V6 diesel and gasoline options are available for drivers who want the combination of performance motoring and people-carrying capacity. Under the skin, too, are seismic changes: the Espace is now entirely metal-bodied, rendering fiberglass a thing of the past for Renault.

New features not fitted to the former Espace include the navigation system with a foldaway screen, rain and sunlight sensors, and an automatic parking brake. More excitement and user-friendliness come from the automatic door opening and closing system, and push-button starting. There are amazingly slim A-pillars to enhance forward visibility, and the largest sunroof available on any car anywhere, with a surface area of 2.16 square meters (23.25 sq ft).

Compared with the previous model, the cabin is subdued but still streamlined, with a slush-molded finish to boost levels of perceived quality. Woven fabrics replace velour; some of the fabrics used for seat upholstery incorporate PVC threads, which add contrast, and combining them with Alcantara brings together a soft sensation and a dry feel.

# Volkswagen Magellan
# Volkswagen Touareg

The recent Touareg SUV has been planned for at Volkswagen for at least five years. It's a car jointly developed with Porsche, and it was this partnership that created the Cayenne for the sports-car firm, and saved a great deal of money for both companies. But what was the point of the Magellan?

Well, Volkswagen has been quietly moving its range upmarket over the past few years; examples of this are the new Passat W8 and Phaeton sedans. Many competitors, even the slow-moving Volvo, now have an SUV in their lineup, so Volkswagen was starting to look behind the times without one of its own, especially as SUVs were proving so popular. The Magellan played an important role in preparing the world for Volkswagen's first SUV. It doesn't look too much like the Touareg, but the proportions are much the same, and the intent is clear: Volkswagen was committed to the market segment.

The final car was a little bigger than the concept and had a Phaeton front-end design rather than the Magellan's cheaper-looking grille and much less impressive headlights. At the rear, the Touareg has a fixed bumper, not split as on the concept; the rear screen is much larger; and the big, bright-red rear lights make the car look tall, with lots of presence. This is all in stark contrast to the insipid architectural approach used on the Magellan at the rear.

The interior is quite luxurious, much like the Phaeton's, and is a complete, and conventional, redesign of the playful, futuristic cabin ideas for the Magellan.

Super-Luxury Cars

# Super-Luxury Cars

Super-luxury, or "super-lux," as the industry has it, means cars with a price of $200,000 and up. It's currently a segment largely dominated by such contrasting brands as Rolls-Royce, Bentley, Ferrari, and Lamborghini. Despite the effects of global uncertainty, plunging stock markets, and the long-gone dot.com bubble, 2003 and 2004 will bring an influx of new super-lux models to choose from, a charge led by the relaunch of some historic brands. The reason for this is the relentless buying-up of historic makes over the past decade. Rolls-Royce, Bentley, Bugatti, and Lamborghini have all been acquired by large German car manufacturers such as BMW and Volkswagen, while DaimlerChrysler has raided its own cellars to revive Maybach, a brand acquired in 1960 and last seen gracing a car in 1941.

It's demographic trends that are luring carmakers into the super-lux segment. There are more and more rich people and their numbers are predicted to grow strongly over the next decade. In the USA alone, sales of super-lux cars are expected to double by 2010 to about six thousand vehicles a year.

Buying such a car sends a strong message to business associates and friends, but manufacturers who offer them are anxious to avoid the negative stigma these cars can attract. In 1936, the number of people in the USA who could afford to buy a Duesenberg was the same as in 1929, but the company's luck ran out: it went out of business because it wasn't considered appropriate to buy, and be seen to own, that kind of car during the Depression. Although many potential customers today may be insulated from short-term economic downturns, if the US economy takes a further prolonged dip, and this in turn affects the Japanese and European markets, there may be a serious shortage of buyers once more.

Volkswagen is the most aggressive of the large carmakers entering the super-lux segment. It now owns Bentley, Bugatti, and Lamborghini. It has also extended the reach of its core Volkswagen and Audi brands upward, and it owns Horch, another historic luxury brand widely rumored to be a candidate for revival. The all-new Bentley Continental GT goes into production at the original plant in Crewe, England, where both Rolls-Royces and Bentleys have traditionally been built. A number of other Bentley derivatives are expected, which is great news for the average Bentley owner, with his or her typical net worth of $14–18 million.

Also owned by VW, Bugatti has been showing its 746-kW (1000-bhp) Veyron concept for the past three years and we are promised this will reach production soon, challenging Ferrari and even the ten-year-old McLaren F1 for the title of the world's fastest car. Lamborghini, meanwhile, is working on new smaller models to extend its brand toward a wider audience, just as Aston Martin is doing with the AMV8 Vantage.

Mercedes-Benz put the Maybach brand into production in 2003. Between the wars, Maybach was one of the world's most exclusive car names, and the Maybach Zeppelin DS 8 was the largest German luxury car of the 1930s. The new model will be manufactured at a rate of fewer than ten units each day, but, in addition to the Maybach, Mercedes-Benz is busy working on the SLR supercar in partnership with McLaren in the UK. The SLR will be made from carbon fiber and aims to be the ultimate aspirational sports car in the Mercedes stable on its launch in 2004.

Rolls-Royce is now owned by BMW, after Volkswagen purchased it and Bentley in 1998. Owing to BMW's previous alliance with Rolls-Royce plc, the jet-engine manufacturer, VW found it did not have the right to use the Rolls-Royce name and so was forced to sell it to its German arch-rival. Roughly three hundred Rolls-Royce cars were sold in 2002, Volkswagen's final, lethargic year as the make's custodian, yet BMW hopes to build six to seven hundred of the new Phantoms in 2003, and eventually to raise annual production to around one thousand. Priced at a cool $332,000, this car offers a range of super-lux details, including a humidified cigar case and door-mounted umbrellas.

But all of these makes provide little financial return. Ford's Aston Martin has revenues of just a few hundred million dollars, by contrast with the $170 billion of Ford itself, and is thought always to have taken a loss. Owning these makes is about industry one-upmanship and confidence in the parent company. Indeed Henry Ford II personally authorized the purchase of Aston Martin in 1987, on a whim, and the Detroit giant is also sitting on British super-lux gems Daimler and Lagonda, both of which could be resurrected. In addition, there are marketing benefits for parent companies merely from the association

**Above**
Aston Martin AMV8 Vantage

**Opposite**
Bentley Continental GT

with an exciting name, as well as the more dubious advantage of having a small-scale operation that can test-manufacture new systems, materials, and designs before these are transferred to mass production with all problems ironed out.

It's not just the Germans and the British who are in on the act. General Motors' Cadillac brand has recently launched two concept cars that show the company is investigating the super-lux arena and pushing Cadillac further upmarket. Both the Cien sports car and the Cadillac Sixteen were designed to compete in this heady segment. GM has studied the business case for both cars, but no decisions have yet been made as to whether Cadillac will join the rest of the fray in frittering away its profits by developing playthings for the restless wealthy.

As a result of all this activity, the super-lux segment now has a competitive feel to it. Still, the key to the market for expensive luxury goods is to keep them exclusive. If the market becomes flooded they simply won't hold their value, and the rich, more than anyone, shun a loser, no matter how exhilarating it is to own.

Technical Glossary

Where the New Models were Launched

Major International Motor Shows 2003–2004

Makes and their Parent Companies

# Technical Glossary

## Specification tables

The following list explains the terminology used in the specification tables that accompany the model descriptions. The amount of data available for any given model depends on its status as a concept or a production car. More information is usually available for models currently in or nearing production.

| | |
|---|---|
| **Engine** | Engine size is quoted in liters, and refers to the swept volume of the cylinders per crankshaft rotation; 6.0, for example, means a 6-liter (or 6000cc) engine.<br><br>"In-line" or "V" followed by a number refers to the engine's number of cylinders. An in-line 4 engine has four cylinders in a single row, while a V8 engine has eight cylinders arranged in a V-formation. In-line engines of more than six cylinders are rare today because they take up too much packaging space—an in-line 12, for instance, would require a very long hood. Only Volkswagen makes a W12, an engine with its twelve cylinders arranged in a W-formation. The configuration of the cylinders is usually chosen on cost grounds: the higher the car's retail price, the more cylinders product planners can include. |
| **Power** | Engine power is given in both metric kilowatts (kW) and imperial brake horsepower (bhp). Both are calculated at optimum engine crankshaft speed, given in "rpm" (revolutions per minute) by manufacturers as a "net" measurement—in other words, an engine's output after power has been sapped by other equipment and the exhaust system—and measured by a "brake" applied to the driveshaft. |
| **Torque** | Simply the motion of twisting or turning, in car terms torque means pulling power, generated by twisting force from the engine crankshaft. It is given in Newton-meters (Nm) and pounds per foot (lb. ft). The better the torque, the more force the engine can apply to the driven wheels. |
| **Gearbox** | This is the mechanical means by which power is transmitted from the engine to the driven wheels. There is a wide variety of manual (with a clutch) and automatic (clutchless) versions. There have been recent trends for clutchless manual systems, called "semi-automatic" or "automated manual," and automatics with an option to change gear manually, sometimes called "Tiptronic," "Steptronic," or "Easytronic." CVT (continuously variable transmission) refers to an automatic with a single "speed": the system uses rubber or steel belts to take engine power to the driven wheels, with drive pulleys that expand and contract to vary the gearing. A "sequential manual" is a manual gearbox with preset gear ratios that are ordered sequentially. |
| **Suspension** | All suspension systems cushion the car against road or terrain conditions to maximize comfort, safety, and road holding. Heavy and off-road vehicles use "rigid axles" at the rear or front and rear; these are suspended using robust, leaf-type springs and steel "wishbones" with "trailing arms." "Semi-rigid axles" are often found at the back on front-wheel-drive cars, in conjunction with a "torsion-beam" trailing-arm axle. "Independent" suspension means each wheel can move up and down on its own, often with the help of "trailing arms" or "semi-trailing arms." A "MacPherson strut," named after its inventor, a Ford engineer called Earl MacPherson, is a suspension upright, fixed to the car's structure above the top of the tire. It carries the wheel hub at the bottom and incorporates a hydraulic damper. It activates a coil spring and, when fitted at the front, turns with the wheel. |

| | |
|---|---|
| Brakes | Almost all modern cars feature disc brakes all round. A few low-powered models still feature drum brakes at the back for cost reasons. "ABS" (anti-lock braking system) is increasingly fitted to all cars: it regulates brake application to prevent the brakes locking in an emergency or slippery conditions. BA (brake assist) is a system that does this electro-hydraulically, while EBD (electronic brake-force distribution) is a pressure regulator that, in braking, spreads the car's weight more evenly so that the brakes do not lock. "ESP" (electronic stability program) is Mercedes-Benz's electronically controlled system that helps keep the car pointing in the right direction at high speeds; sensors detect wayward road holding and apply the brakes indirectly to correct it. "Dynamic stability" is a similar system. "Brake-by-wire" is a totally electronic braking system that sends signals from brake pedal to brakes with no mechanical actuation whatsoever. "TCS" (traction-control system) is a feature that holds acceleration slip within acceptable levels to prevent wheel-spin and therefore improves adhesion to the road. "VSC" (vehicle stability control) is the computer-controlled application of anti-lock braking to all four wheels individually to prevent dangerous skidding during cornering. |
| Tires | The size and type of wheels and tires are given in the internationally accepted formula. Representative examples include: 315/70R17, 235/50VR18, 225/50WR17, 235/40Z18, and 225/40ZR18. In all cases, the number before the slash is the tire width in millimeters. The number after the slash is the height-to-width ratio of the tire section as a percentage. The letter R denotes radial construction. Letters preceding R are a guide to the tire's speed rating, denoting the maximum safe operating speed. H tires can be used at speeds up to 210 km/h (130 mph), V up to 240 km/h (150 mph), W up to 270 km/h (170 mph), and Y up to 300 km/h (190 mph). Finally, the last number is the diameter of the wheel in inches. A PAX is a wheel-and-tire in one unit, developed by Michelin (for example, 19/245 PAX means a 19-in. wheel with a 245-mm tire width). The rubber tire element is clipped to the steel wheel part, rather than held on by pressure. The height of the tire walls is reduced, which can free up space for better internal packaging, or for bigger wheels for concept-car looks. It can also run flat for 200 km at 80 km/h, eliminating the need for a spare. |
| Wheelbase | The exact distance between the center of the front wheel and the center of the rear wheel. |
| Track front/rear | The exact distance between the center of the front or rear tires, measured across the car at the ground. |
| Curb weight | The amount a car weighs with a tank of fuel, all oils and coolants topped off, and all standard equipment but no occupants. |
| $CO_2$ emissions | Carbon-dioxide emissions, which are a direct result of fuel consumption. $CO_2$ contributes to the atmospheric "greenhouse effect." Less than 100 g/km is a very low emission, 150 g/km is good, 300 g/km is bad. "PZEV" (partial zero emission vehicle) refers to a low-level emission standard that was created to allow flexibility on ZEV standards in California. |

## Other terms

| | |
|---|---|
| A-, B-, C-, D-pillars | Vertical roof-support posts that form part of a car's bodywork. The A-pillar sits between windshield and front door, the B-pillar between front and rear doors, the C-pillar between rear doors and rear window, hatchback, or estate rear-side windows, and the D-pillar (on an estate) between rear side windows and tailgate. Confusingly, however, some designs refer to the central pillar between front and rear doors as a B-pillar, where it faces the front door, and a C-pillar, where it faces the rear one. |

| | |
|---|---|
| Cant rail | The structural beam that runs along the tops of the doors. |
| Coefficient of drag | Also known as the Cd, this is shorthand for the complex scientific equation that proves how aerodynamic a car is. The Citroën C-Airdream, for example, has a Cd of 0.28, but the Citroën SM of thirty years ago measured just 0.24, so it is not exactly rocket science any more. Drag means the resistance of a body to airflow, and low drag means better penetration, less friction, and therefore more efficiency, although sometimes poor dynamic stability. |
| Drive-by-wire technology | Increasingly featured on new cars, these systems do away with mechanical elements and replace them by wires transmitting electronic signals to activate functions such as brakes and steering. |
| Drivetrain | The assembly of "organs" that gives a car motive power: engine, gearbox, driveshaft, wheels, brakes, suspension, and steering. This grouping is also loosely known these days as a chassis, and can be transplanted into several different models to save on development costs. |
| Feature line | A styling detail usually added to a design to differentiate it from its rivals, and generally not related to functional areas such as door apertures. |
| Greenhouse | Car-design slang for the glazed area of the passenger compartment that usually sits above the car's waist level. |
| Instrument panel | The trim panel that sits in front of the driver and front passenger. |
| Monospace/ Monovolume/"one-box" | A "box" is one of the major volumetric components of a car's architecture. In a traditional sedan, there are three boxes: one for the engine, one for the passengers, and one for the luggage. A hatchback, missing a trunk, is a "two-box" car, while a large MPV such as the Renault Espace is a "one-box" design, also known as a "monospace" or "monovolume." |
| MPV | Short for "multi-purpose vehicle," and applied to tall, spacious cars that can carry at least five passengers, and often as many as nine, or versatile combinations of people and cargo. The 1983 Chrysler Voyager and 1984 Renault Espace were the first. The 1977 Matra Rancho was the very first "mini-MPV," but the 1991 Mitsubishi Space Runner was the first in the modern idiom. |
| Packaging space | Any three-dimensional zone in a vehicle that is occupied by component parts or used during operation of the vehicle. |
| Platform | The invisible, but elemental and expensive, basic structure of a modern car. It is the task of contemporary car designers to achieve maximum aesthetic diversity from a single platform. |
| Powertrain | The engine, gearbox, and transmission "package" of a car. |
| Spaceframe | A structural frame that supports a car's mechanical systems and cosmetic panels. |
| SUV | Short for "sports utility vehicle," a four-wheel-drive car designed for leisure off-road driving but not necessarily agricultural or industrial use. Therefore a Land Rover Defender is not an SUV, while a Land Rover Freelander is. The line between the two is sometimes difficult to draw, and identifying a pioneer is tricky: SUVs as we know them today were defined by Jeep in 1986 with the Wrangler, Suzuki in 1988 with the Vitara, and Daihatsu in 1989 with the Sportrak. |
| Targa | Porsche had been very successful in the Targa Florio road races in Sicily, so, in celebration, in 1965, the company applied the name "Targa" (the Italian for shield) to a new 911 model that featured a novel detachable roof panel. It is now standard terminology for the system, although a Porsche-registered trademark. |
| Telematics | Any individual communication to a car from an outside base station, for example, satellite navigation signals, automatic emergency calls, roadside assistance, traffic information, and dynamic route guidance. |

### Non-motorshow debut

14 April 2002 at Volkswagen, Wolfsburg, Germany

**Concept**

Volkswagen L1

### New York International Auto Show

29 March – 7 April 2002

**Production**

Chrysler Pacifica
Honda Element
Infiniti M45
Lincoln Aviator
Nissan Murano
Saturn Ion

### Paris Motor Show (Mondial de l'automobile)

28 September – 13 October 2002

**Concept**

Bentley Continental GT
Chrysler California Cruiser
Citroën C-Airdream
GM Hy-wire
Kia KCV-II
Peugeot H$_2$O
Peugeot Sésame
Renault Ellypse
Sivax Streetster Kira

**Production**

Audi A8
BMW Z4
Ferrari Enzo
Ford Streetka
Honda Accord
Jaguar XJ
Maybach
Mazda2
MCC Smart Roadster/Roadster-Coupé
Nissan Micra
Opel Meriva
Porsche Cayenne
Renault Espace
Renault Mégane
Saab 9-3
Seat Cordoba
Toyota Land Cruiser
Volkswagen Touareg

### British International Motor Show

23 October – 3 November 2002

**Production**

Invicta S1
MG XPower SV
TVR T350

### Seoul Motor Show

21–29 November 2002

**Concept**

Daewoo Flex
Hyundai HIC

**Production**

Daewoo Nubira

### International Car and Motorcycle Exhibition,

Bologna
7–15 December 2002

**Concept**

Fiat Simba

### Greater LA Auto Show

4–12 January 2003

**Concept**

Dodge Magnum SRT-8
Ford Faction

**Production**

Scion xA
Scion xB

### North American International Auto Show (NAIAS)

Detroit
11–20 January 2003

**Concept**

Aston Martin AMV8 Vantage
Audi Pikes Peak
BMW xActivity
Buick Centieme
Cadillac Sixteen
Chevrolet Cheyenne
Chevrolet SS
Dodge Avenger
Dodge Durango
Dodge Kahuna
Ford 427
Ford Freestyle FX
Ford Model U
Ford Mustang GT
Infiniti Triant
Kia KCD-1 Slice
Lincoln Navicross
Matra P75
Mazda Washu
Mercury Messenger
Mitsubishi Tarmac Spyder
Pontiac G6

### Production

Acura TSX
Cadillac SRX
Chevrolet Colorado
Chevrolet Equinox
Chevrolet Malibu
Ford F-150
Infiniti FX45
Lexus RX330
Mitsubishi Endeavor
Nissan Maxima
Nissan Quest
Nissan Titan
Pontiac Grand Prix
Rolls-Royce Phantom
Toyota Sienna

### Chicago Auto Show

14–23 February 2003

**Production**

Chevrolet Aveo
Ford Freestar
Mercury Monterey
Suzuki Forenza
Suzuki Verona

### 73rd Geneva International Motor Show

6–16 March 2003

**Concept**

Alfa Romeo Kamal
Audi Nuvolari
Bertone Birusa
Chrysler Airflite
Daewoo Scope
Fiat Marrakech
Italdesign Moray
Mazda MX Sportif
Nissan Evalia
Opel GTC Genève
Peugeot Hoggar
Pininfarina Enjoy
Rinspeed Bedouin
Subaru B11S Coupé
Volvo VCC

**Production**

Audi A3
Fiat Gingo
Fiat Idea
Ford Focus C-Max
Lamborghini Gallardo
Lancia Ypsilon
Opel Signum
Renault Scénic 2

# Major International Motor Shows 2003–2004

**Paris Motor Show**
**(Mondial de l'automobile)**
Sunday 28 September – Monday 13 October 2003
Paris Expo, Paris, France
www.mondialauto.tm.fr

**Budapest Motor Show**
Tuesday 14 – Sunday 19 October 2003
Budapest Fair Center, Budapest, Hungary
www.automobil.hungexpo.hu

**Prague Auto Show (Autoshow Praha)**
Thursday 16 – Sunday 19 October 2003
Prague Exhibition Grounds, Prague,
Czech Republic
www.incheba.cz

**Tokyo Motor Show**
Saturday 25 October – Wednesday 5 November
2003
Nippon Convention Center, Chiba City, Tokyo
www.tokyo-motorshow.com

**Riyadh Motor Show**
Sunday 9 – Friday 14 November 2003
Riyadh Exhibition Center, Riyadh, Saudi Arabia
www.recexpo.com

**Middle East International Motor Show**
Thursday 11 – Monday 15 December 2003
Dubai World Trade Center (DWTC), Dubai,
United Arab Emirates
www.dubaimotorshow.com

**Greater LA Auto Show**
Friday 2 – Sunday 11 January 2004
Los Angeles Convention Center, Los Angeles, USA
www.laautoshow.com

**North American International Auto Show**
**(NAIAS)**
Saturday 10 – Monday 19 January 2004
Cobo Center, Detroit, USA
www.naias.com

**Brussels International Motor Show**
Thursday 15 – Sunday 25 January 2004
Brussels Expo, Brussels, Belgium
www.febiac.be/motorshows

**Chicago Auto Show**
Friday 6 – Sunday 15 February 2004
McCormick Place South, Chicago, USA
www.chicagoautoshow.com

**Canadian International Auto Show**
Friday 13 – Sunday 22 February 2004
Metro Toronto Convention Centre and SkyDome,
Toronto, Canada
www.autoshow.ca

**Melbourne International Motor Show**
Thursday 26 February – Monday 8 March 2004
Melbourne Exhibition Centre, Melbourne,
Australia
www.motorshow.com.au

**74th Geneva International Motor Show**
Thursday 4 – Sunday 14 March 2004
Palexpo, Geneva, Switzerland
www.salon-auto.ch

**Tallinn Motor Show (Motorex 2004)**
Wednesday 24 – Sunday 28 March 2004
The Estonian Fairs Center
Tallinn, Estonia
www.fair.ee

**New York International Auto Show**
Friday 9 – Sunday 18 April 2004
The Jacob Javits Convention Center,
New York, USA
www.autoshowny.com

**British International Motor Show**
Tuesday 25 May – Sunday 6 June 2004
National Exhibition Centre (NEC), Birmingham, UK
www.motorshow.co.uk

**Paris Motor Show**
**(Mondial de l'automobile)**
Saturday 2 – Sunday 17 October 2004
Paris Expo, Paris, France
www.mondialauto.tm.fr

# Makes and their Parent Companies

Hundreds of separate car-making companies have consolidated over the past decade into ten groups: General Motors, Ford, DaimlerChrysler, VW, Toyota, Peugeot, Renault, BMW, Honda, and Hyundai. These account for at least nine of every ten cars produced globally today.

The remaining independent makes either produce specialist models, offer niche design and engineering services, or tend to be at risk because of their lack of economies of scale.

The general global improvement in vehicle quality means manufacturers would be wise to continue to rely heavily on design to differentiate their brands.

**BMW**
BMW
Mini
Riley*
Rolls-Royce
Triumph*

**DaimlerChrysler**
Chrysler
De Soto*
Dodge
Hudson*
Imperial*
Jeep
Maybach
Mercedes-Benz
Mitsubishi
Nash*
Plymouth*
Smart

**Fiat Auto**
Abarth*
Alfa Romeo
Autobianchi*
Ferrari
Fiat
Innocenti*
Lancia
Maserati

**Ford**
Aston Martin
Daimler
Ford
Jaguar
Lagonda*
Land Rover
Lincoln

Mazda
Mercury
Range Rover
Th!nk*
Volvo

**General Motors**
Buick
Cadillac
Chevrolet
Daewoo
GMC
Holden
Hummer
Isuzu
Oldsmobile*
Opel
Pontiac
Saab
Saturn
Subaru
Suzuki
Vauxhall

**Honda**
Acura
Honda

**Hyundai**
Asia Motors
Hyundai
Kia

**MG Rover**
Austin*
MG
Morris*
Rover
Wolseley*

**Peugeot**
Citroën
Hillman*
Humber*
Panhard*
Peugeot
Simca*
Singer*
Sunbeam*
Talbot*

**Proton**
Lotus
Proton

**Renault**
Alpine*
Dacia
Datsun*
Infiniti
Nissan
Renault
Renault Sport

**Toyota**
Daihatsu
Lexus
Toyota

**VW**
Audi
Auto Union*
Bentley
Bugatti
Cosworth
DKW*
Horch*
Lamborghini
NSU*

Seat
Skoda
Volkswagen
Wanderer*

**Independent makes**
Austin-Healey*
Bertone
Bristol
Caterham
Fioravanti
Heuliez
Invicta
Irmscher
Italdesign
Lada
Koenigsegg
Matra
Mitsuoka
Morgan
Pininfarina
Porsche
Rinspeed
Sivax
SsangYong
Tata
TVR
Venturi
Westfield
Zagato

* Dormant makes

# Picture Credits

The illustrations in this book have been reproduced with the kind permission of the following manufacturers:

Alfa Romeo
Aston Martin Lagonda
Audi AG
Bentley Motors
Bertone SpA
BMW AG
Buick
Cadillac
Chevrolet
Citroën
GM Daewoo Motors
DaimlerChrysler
Dodge
Ferrari SpA
Fiat Auto
Ford Motor Company
General Motors Corporation

Honda Motor Co
Hyundai Car UK
Invicta Car Company
Italdesign
Jaguar Cars
Kia Motors Corporation
Automobili Lamborghini
Lancia
Lincoln
Matra
Mazda Motors
Mercury
MG Rover Group
Mitsubishi Motors Corporation
Nissan Motors
Opel AG
Peugeot SA

Pininfarina SpA
Pontiac
Porsche AG
Renault SA
Rinspeed
Rolls-Royce Motor Cars
Saab Automobile AB
Saturn
Seat SA
Sivax
Subaru
Suzuki Motor Corporation
Toyota Motor Corporation
TVR Engineering
Volkswagen AG
Volvo Car Corporation

# Acknowledgments

I would firstly like to thank everyone at Merrell Publishers who has helped ensure that *The Car Design Yearbook 1* was such a fabulous success, and for their commitment to building on that success for future editions. I would especially like to thank Anthea Snow, Kate Ward, Emily Sanders, and Emilie Nangle.

Thanks are also due to the manufacturers' press offices, which have been extremely supportive once again in providing technical and photographic material. I would like to thank Vicky Gallagher for her continual support, and Peter Newbury for his assistance in researching the technical specifications. I must also thank Giles Chapman and Richard Dawes for their professional editorial support, and Alistair Layzell for his success in the public-relations campaign.

Stephen Newbury
Henley-on-Thames, Oxfordshire
2003